ROVE
DRIVERS

TECHNICAL TIPS
THE FIRST 25 YEARS

ISBN 0 948706 15 5

Published by Brent Publications

Printed by
Basildon Printing Company Limited,
Fleet House,
Armstrong Road,
South Benfleet,
Essex,
SS7 4FH

To celebrate the first twenty-five years of the Rover P4 Drivers Guild, we thought it would be a good idea to publish a comprehensive selection of the Technical articles that have appeared in the pages of 'Overdrive' since the inception of the Guild in 1977 up to 2002.

I am sure that even you founder members out there will not mind re-reading these really useful hints and tips, but of course, our newer membership will benefit from the past knowledge that they have missed.

Whilst compiling the various articles, I realised, sadly, that some of the authors are no longer with us, but they have left us with the legacy of their knowledge.

The articles are reprinted from the originals, so some of the prices and telephone numbers may well be of no relevance, but apart from that, I am sure you will find some extremely worthwhile advice to keep your P4 in good mechanical order.

I am sure you will enjoy reading this book and join with us in wishing the Rover P4 Drivers Guild a very happy future.

Stan Johnstone

Press Release Photo – September 1949

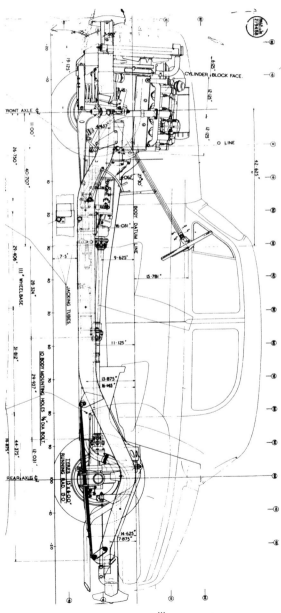

DECARBONISATION AND TOP END OVERHAUL

The following instructions apply to '95', '100' and '110' models in particular, although all six cylinder models are basically similar.

1. Disconnect battery. Set heater controls to "off" position.
2. Remove radiator cap and drain coolant from radiator, and engine block. There is a tap under radiator offside, another one offside of engine block. Use a length of hose pipe on the latter to save soaking the engine compartment.
3. Remove the air silencer/cleaner or oil bath and intake elbow.
4. Remove the flexible air hose to top of carburettor float chamber, the petrol feed pipe and the cold start control cable. Do not lose the small grub screw securing the latter.
5. Disconnect the radiator top hose and the brake air servo pipe at the cylinder head.
6. Disconnect the wiring from the ignition coil, mixture control switch and the low tension lead from the distributor; remove the spark plug leads, distributor cap and ignition leads in one unit. Remove vacuum pipe from distributor, ignition coil and metal cover from above the cooling fan.
7. Take off the alloy heat shield and metal heater pipe from the exhaust manifold. (Note the position of nuts and spacers as this can be forgotten on re-assembly)
8. Remove the top rocker cover and gasket, then the oil feed pipe at rear of cylinder head. Unscrew the thermometer bulb from the cylinder head on '100' models (this may be stubborn, and on no account damage the wire wound tube although this must be gently bent out of the way). On '95' and '100' models pull off the connector.
9. Slacken off the two pinch bolts on the carburettor flexible coupling. Undo the carburettor securing nuts and remove the instrument complete. Do not lose the return spring or choke cable support bracket.
10. Remove the distributor locating bolt and lift out the unit. To ensure correct replacement, scribe a line on the clamp flange and mounting point. Do not slacken the pinch bolt.
11. Undo the three nuts securing the exhaust pipe to the manifold and pull down the pipe. Undo the manifold securing nuts and clamps and remove exhaust manifold.
12. Remove spark plugs.

13. Slacken the inlet tappets right off.
14. Undo the cylinder head securing bolts in the reverse order of assembly, progressively, (see diagram p.3) in order to avoid distortion.
15. Removal of the head is made easier if a wooden handle (old broom handle is suitable) is made to fit over the rocker studs and secured by nuts. The weight is considerable. There will be no difficulty in removing the head but take care to see that the pushrods are left behind in the block or they may fall as the head is lifted.
16. Remove pushrods and retain in their original order (use an inverted cardboard box with six holes).
17. Remove side rocker cover and gasket.
18. On '110' models the rocker gear lifts off as one unit after removal of the securing nuts. On '95' and '100' models, take off the nuts, washers and retaining plates on the thrust blocks, shaft locating screws and end plug. The rocker shafts may be withdrawn using a soft metal drift or hardwood dowel (unless you have extractor Part No. 263749). Note the position of all oil holes for re-assembly, and retain all parts in their original sequences.

Decarbonisation/Valve Removal

19. Remove all carbon from the top of each piston crown using a soft scraper. Work on each piston at top dead centre and wipe off carbon with an oily rag as it is loosened. Stuff some rag into each bore to prevent ingress of dirt.

Inlet Valves

20. Remove valves using a strong spring compressor, do not overtighten. A tap downwards on the valve retaining caps to free the split cones will be necessary. Prise out the split cones and keep in their original pairs. Retain the valves in sequence also. There will be a thick oily deposit on the valve heads and stems; clean this off with a soft scraper. It is essential to remove the old valve guide seals since these harden with age and are responsible for excess oil being burnt. Be sure to get them out and clean the locating grooves. Grind in the inlet valves using fine grinding paste until a uniform seating is evident on the valve and valve seat, about 1/16" - 3/32" thick. Excessive grinding should not be necessary. Clean the valves, guides and ports with paraffin. Push new valve seats down the guides, making sure

they seat correctly in their grooves. Insert the clean valves gently (oil the stems first); replace springs, valve caps and split cones using the spring compressor. (Note: on '110' models it is not necessary to remove the inlet manifold for this overhaul.)

Exhaust Valves

21. All the six cylinder engines run "hot" on the side exhaust valves and a good grinding, clean up and even renewal will be required after 50,000 - 70,000 miles, depending on use.

   Slacken the tappets right off and use the starting handle to turn the engine over until the compressor can be used on each valve in turn. Use a blob of grease on top of the split cones to keep them from falling down into the sump (if this happens, you are in trouble). Carbon deposits on the valves will be hard and persistent scraping is required. The valve seats are less likely to be in poor condition. Grind in, clean, oil and replace as for the inlet valves. The mating surfaces should be a little wider, however, - about ⅛".

Head Replacement

22. Replace pushrods. Smear a new gasket (marked "This side up") with oil and place on block. Use two metal rods or studs at either end to assist in head location. Make sure the thermostat bypass hose ('95' and '100' models) or rubber sealing ring ('110' models) are correctly positioned. Tighten the cylinder head bolts evenly and in order shown (essential) to the following torques:

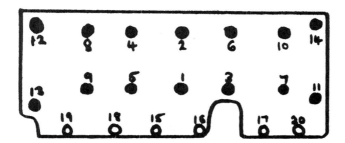

●　　Bolts 'A' – 50 ft.lbs.
○　　Bolts 'B' – 30 ft.lbs.

Set tappets to:

	LATE P4		EARLY P4
inlet	·006"		·008"
exhaust	·010"		·012"

23. Refit all components in reverse order of removal, but before replacing spark plugs, squirt some clean engine oil into each cylinder and turn over several times on the handle. Make sure the exhaust manifold and faces are clean and use new gaskets, steel face towards manifold. Ignition timing will not need resetting if the distributor is replaced exactly as found (use the scribe marks) since it is impossible to locate this item back to front. Choke operation is dependent on the correct positioning of the grub screw securing point but this too should not have been disturbed.

24. Refill radiator, start engine and check for leaks. Tappets will need resetting when hot. Make sure to re-check head bolts to correct torques after 500 miles.

May 1977

Richard J. Ginger

P4 UPHOLSTERY - RESTORATION

If the surface of the leather has been scratched or abrased the affected parts should be treated with coloured lacquer. In some cases, it suffices to "touch-in" the damaged parts with the lacquer, which can be applied by a suitable brush or swab. If it becomes necessary to treat the entire surface of a seat with the coloured lacquer, the directions are as follows:

Having made sure the leather is thoroughly dry (after washing) -

STIR THE LACQUER WELL BEFORE USING.

Pour a small quantity into a shallow container and, dipping a swab of stockinette into the lacquer, apply evenly and sparingly to the leather. If necessary a further coat can be applied after the first has dried.

A second coat can be applied by spray for a more even finish.

Carry out the above renovation in a warm dry shop, or in warm dry weather, this will prevent blushing.

Cleaning Instructions

Waterproof coloured finishes such as "Vaumol" brand – wash the leather thoroughly with warm water and pure non-caustic soap, (Glycerine) or with Connolly's Concentrated Cleaner.

If the Concentrated Cleaner is used, proceed as follows:

Make a solution of one part of cleaner to twelve parts of warm water (the cleaner must not be used in its concentrated form).

Immerse a soft cloth in this solution, wring out the cloth and rub lightly the surface to be cleaned. Avoid flooding and change the surface of the cloth frequently.

In order to remove any residue, repeat the operation with a fresh cloth damped with clean water. Dry well with a soft cloth.

A small brush such as a nail brush (not too hard) can be used to remove dirt which has become ingrained in cushions or the top and corners of the seat.

Connolly Bros

July 1977

NOTES ON YOUR P4 CHASSIS

The Rover P4 chassis is not as sound as it may first appear (what blasphemy! - ed.) It is prone to serious rotting in a few places. All these potential trouble spots are at the rear and can be listed as follows:

(1)   Under spare wheel carriers, top of chassis.

(2)   Inside chassis side wall, both sides, from petrol tank support bar to rear shackle and forward of petrol tank support bar to shock absorber mounting.

(3)   Outside chassis side wall from rear jacking post to rear axle bump stop.

(4)   Under chassis bump stop mounting - both sides.

(5)   End of chassis outer side wall at rear end.

(6)   Either side of rear bumper bracket mounting plate on top of chassis - both sides.

Corrosion usually sets in from the outside and if work is undertaken and executed properly, it should be possible to repair the chassis. Although a hole may appear, experience has shown that within ¼" of the edge of the hole on the inside one may still find the original black paint covering completely rust free metal (i.e. inside of box section).

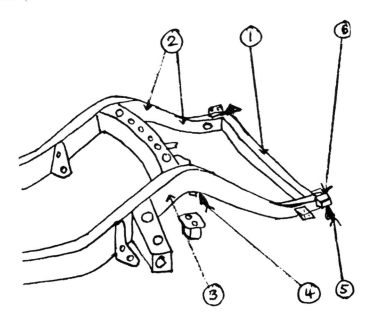

Rust Fighting

Once rust has started to eat away at metal it is almost impossible to stop it unless it is sand blasted. However, the process can be slowed down. Being unable to find an adequately effective neutralizer or rust killer, I prefer to do the following. I prepare the surface in the normal way and paint a Calcium Plumbate lead based priming paint, which is also a rust inhibitor (BS 3698 type A) called 'Rustodian'. It soaks into the rust infected metal and, after one coat the surface is ready for a top coat. I then apply the old fashioned 2-4 hour lacquer called 'Valspar'. It is now marketed in a new style tin - only one coat is required; it dries within hours leaving a glossy finish second to none.

Replacing Rear Springs

If the original springs are old and rusty (flat) throw them away as they will not contain enough steel to be tampered and re-set. The cost of adding new leaves to give them sufficient strength will be more than the cost of new springs. Difficulty may be encountered when slackening the six shackle self locking nuts, however if you apply the blow-lamp technique you will probably win.

The rear-axle 'U' bolts are difficult to separate from the shock absorber mounting brackets - they cost approx. £2 each. I had to admit defeat and replaced them after removing the old ones with a hacksaw and chisel. Incidentally, they were only removed afterwards by drilling out the mounting brackets. Not mentioned in the manuals, here is a tip worth remembering: The stop brackets bolted onto the chassis can be removed and there is no need to lever the spring into position as the shackles and spring fall into place. The bracket can be fitted with the car standing on two wheels with springs partially compressed by the weight of the car. Another point is that the six bolts - 3 per side - are all different and cannot be interchanged. Everything else should be straightforward.

J H Godfrey

October 1977

WINDOW FRAMES

One of the difficulties about writing articles, I have just discovered, is how to start them off. However, I am started now and I hope all the members of Overdrive will forgive any faults they may find, letting me know if they find better ways of doing things, or more particularly, any errors. I am trying to write the article for the complete novice and yet perhaps have a helpful hint even for those who are far more knowledgeable than I. My articles are based on actual work I have recently carried out on my own Rover - a Rover '60' made in 1956 - and will always have a bias towards doing it yourself as cheaply as possible.

One of the problems with the wooden window frames after many years is that the shellac coating put on at the factory becomes chipped and discoloured. A new coat improves the appearance considerably.

Removal of Frame

If you look at Fig. 1 (p.10) you will see that the frame is attached to the metal of the door at six points, (A.B.C.D.E and F). A. and B. are two screws in the front edge of the door when it is open. C.D.E. and F. are half inch self-tapping screws. These are the awkward ones! Firstly, find a screwdriver which fits the slot on the screw head perfectly - these screws are sometimes very tight and it is easy to spoil the head - a long screwdriver, i.e. an electricians' type is helpful because your hand does not cover what you are doing. I had better explain here that finding the screws is a little like looking for a needle in a haystack. Wind down the window, consult Fig. 1 and if you try, say, screw F. (the easiest to find) you will have some idea what you are looking for. The screw is often hidden behind the felt in the bottom or back of the window channel. If it is obviously rusted in to the metal then use one of the usual rust releasers, such as Plus-gas, and leave to soak. Make sure your screwdriver is properly engaged in the screw head, press hard and turn; if very difficult try tightening the screw just a fraction to get the threads free. I was fortunate in that all the screws came out, except three, without too much damage to the slot in the head. On the ones with damage to the slot I was lucky and a larger size of screwdriver blade started them moving and I changed back to the smaller screwdriver to finish them off. If you do damage the slot too badly, it is more than likely that it will be impossible to drill the head off as the screws are very hard. In this case I can only suggest you take out all the other screws, ease the frame away from the door and try to get a small hacksaw blade between the window channel and the door frame to saw through the screw which is shown in Fig. 3 at x. Some damage to the frame and door is bound to result so it is essential you get the screws out the normal way if at all possible. The rear door is just the same as the front door except that screws A. and B. are in the window channel (G. and H. in Fig. 2). Re-glue any loose joints, if necessary, tightening them with a countersunk screw through the joint but not out the other side. Make sure the frame stays in alignment.

Treating the Frame

The frame is sprayed at the factory with some sort of shellac which gives the wood an even coloured finish, and I have not discovered what product this is. Can anybody help? In view of this I decided to use Sanderson's Translac Clear Polyurethane, obtainable from any D.I.Y. shop. I knew this would bring out the colour and grain of the wood and not produce the same even colouring as original, so any purists will have to forgive me. The finished Translac can, when thoroughly hard, be lightly compounded with cellulose rubbing compound to correct any minor blemishes and improve the polish. Take care when removing the old shellac that you work only in the direction of the grain of the wood and that you do not stress the joints in the frame by leaning or pressing too hard. Work on one section of frame, between joints, at a time, being careful not to overlap the joint as the next section's grain goes in a different way. Scores, scratches and scraping show up like a sore thumb in the finished frame, especially if they go a different way to the grain. I personally, used a coarse sandpaper to score the old finish and then carefully scraped each section with an old but reasonably sharp Stanley blade and found that the old finish came off fairly easily. Any marks or old finish which had been left or unnoticed, show up if you paint the frame with turps. This gives you an idea what colour the finished frame will be. Let the frame dry out and correct any marks, particularly removing old finish as it shows badly under Translac. I had to rub one frame down again! By the way, painting with turps, also removes any dust particles. Give the frame two coats of Translac as per instructions on the tin. You will find the frame has sound-deadening felts stuck on and these can be renewed or replaced if necessary. Treat any rusty brackets with a rust killer after removing them from the frame. Clean with appropriate solvent and then spray the bracket with matt black.

Replacing the Frame

Replacement is common sense; just reverse the removal procedure, but a couple of hints are to offer the frame up to the door and mark the door flange with tape where the brackets slot between the window channel and door. Push frame home carefully to check fit, if joints have needed attention, because the brackets disappear when the frame is pushed home and, at least, you will have some idea whereabouts to look in the window channel for the screw holes. Replace any screws which look even slightly suspect because, if in the future you need to get to your door locks or window winders, the window frames have to be removed before you can remove the upholstery panel on the inside of the door. One more point, remember to lightly smear the screws C. to H. with grease as the post 1959 Rovers had metal doors, not alloy doors like the earlier models.

Do not forget a tin or box for the screws before you start.

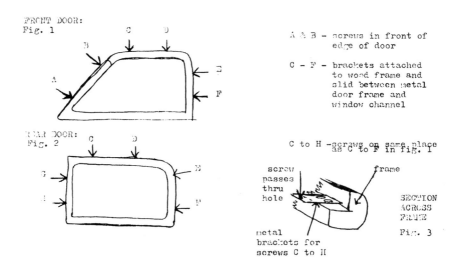

Well, I think I have covered almost everything and, now you have read the articles, if you do decide to do this job, try to incorporate with any repairs to the locks etc. I hope to write an article on the rest of the woodwork, also removal of the door insides soon but, if you are desperate, ring me at Brigg 53351 any evening, Monday to Friday, after about 7p.m. (leave a telephone number if I am out).

Peter M. Wilkinson   *January 1978*

WINDOW FRAMES:

Peter Wilkinson's article in Issue 5 sparked off much written discussion and the reactions of various members follows.

Chris Paling writes: (Chris prefers the orthodox terms and calls them window 'mouldings')

1. I would not advise the use of varnish for when the moulding is heated by the sun and magnified through the glass it will cause the air trapped under the varnish to expand causing blistering or bubbles in the varnish.

2. Rover recommends the following:
    Preparation
    1) Strip the moulding by immersion in cellulose thinners for 5-6 hours or until the original polish is soft.
    2) Scour with wire wool to remove all traces of polish.
    3) Leave to dry for 30 minutes.
    4) Remove surface damage from the moulding with a fine grade sandpaper applied along the grain of the wood.

3. **Staining**
    either
    1) Rub burnt turkey umber mixed with turpentine into the grain of the wood; apply with a rag.
    2) Leave to dry for 30 minutes until the stain powders.
    3) Remove the powder with a clean dry rag.
    or spray with cellulose walnut stain to desired colour and leave to dry for one hour.

4. **Spraying with clear lacquer**
    1) Thin the clear lacquer - not stronger than one part lacquer to two parts of thinners.
    2) Spray with five coats of thinned lacquer allowing 30 minutes drying between coats.
    3) Thin further lacquer to 50% with thinners.
    4) Spray ten to twelve further coats, again allowing 30 minutes drying between coats.
    5) Allow to dry for as long as possible before polishing - at least 48 hours.

5. **Finishing**
    1) Flat to a smooth matt surface using No. 320 wet & dry paper dipped in turps. Care must be taken not to rub through the lacquer on the edges of the moulding.
    2) Polish with a fine rubbing compound using a soft cloth rubbing well in straight lines. Do not use a rotary polishing action.
    3) Finish with a good wax polish applied with a slightly damp cloth.

One of my window frames was apart on the joint and was starting to split along the middle with the grain of the wood. I was advised to put plenty of woodworking adhesive (Evo-stik) on both sides and press together, then sandpaper over the crack when the glue dries. The adhesive becomes clear when hard and the wood-dust settles into the glue. One could not detect the crack afterwards.

I applied clear-gloss varnish mixing in dye (teak) and the result was excellent I thinned the varnish 50/50 with a recommended thinners and applied six coats with a brush rubbing it down with steel wool between applications. The frames look like new now.

Ian Burns writes:

My P4 '100' had been standing for two years with the windows open and therefore the window frames were in a bad way. The front ones had come asunder. After removing the frames, remove the French polish. This can easily be done with a sharp plane blade, using it as a scraper and with the cap iron removed. Also clean up the back of the wood as damp gets in there soaking through the frame causing the finish to be destroyed. Then sand with a fine grade paper. Apply a coat of polyurethane, on the back too, and allow to dry. Sand and apply another two coats. Then finish with wire wool and a good brand of wax polish. This produces an ultra-smooth finish with a semi-gloss shine. The coating of polyurethane on the back wall prevents damp spoiling the finish.

Any pieces that need glueing can be assembled now using "Cascamite" - a waterproof resin glue. If necessary make strips to fit in the slots at the end and when dry excess glue can be chipped off with a sharp chisel. Once replaced in the car the wood can be re-waxed. The best finish is obtained by removing the shine with wire wool and wax, and polishing with a soft rag.

J Butterworth adds that Blackfriar Polyurethane P100 semi-gloss clear varnish gives a preferable subdued finish compared with "Translac". Rubbing down is 95% of the work however, and it is also important to remember to stir the varnish well otherwise it will come out as gloss - the matt particles sit at the bottom:

Another possibly unorthodox approach came through from **Ian Gough**:

While admitting that the right way to set about this job is to remove the frame from the door I managed quite successfully with the frame 'in situ'. The attempts to locate and remove the screws can create more problems and do more damage than the exercise is worth. In addition, if the frame is removed, the joints are often so 'ripe' that it is impossible to prepare the wood for re-varnishing without 'breaking' the frame and then reconstructing the joints.

This is what I do:

I mesh all the adjacent metal and door panel as well as the quarter light. I wind the window right down and then mesh the protruding glass. Trying to remove the varnish coating with sand paper proved to be very expensive both in terms of sand paper and blisters. However, application of sparing amounts of Car Plan paint stripper lifts the top coat very quickly. Provided it is used sparingly this stripper dries as it is scraped off so there is no problem of where and where not to put a sticky, destructive jelly! Instead the dried mixture can be caught in the hand or blown away. Contrary to the instructions on the tin I have found no need to neutralise the surfaces with water before painting.

Once the bulk of the varnish has been removed in this way sanding can remove the rest very quickly. I then coat the wood with 3-4 coats of very thin polyurethane varnish allowing overnight drying between coats followed by two coats of very thin gloss finish polyurethane varnish, meaning 50% thinners and 50% varnish. This brings up the wood grain beautifully and produces a high gloss and durable finish. While allowing the varnish to dry, at least to the 'touch dry' state, do not shut the car door otherwise the furry door piping moults all over your varnish!

Two final notes: when trying to replace a split window frame I was quoted.... wait for it.... £20 by Roverpart of Lewisham and £2 by 'Rover Spares'. This does not appear to be an isolated case....

Returning to the renovation problem - there was an excellent article in the December '77 issue of Thoroughbred and Classic Car.

I.G.

July 1978

13

FRONT SUSPENSION TOP LINK BUSH REPLACEMENT

Jim Hood of Brentwood originally sent in some notes on this and **Peter Rickinson** added his observations too:

Having just replaced very worn suspension bushes on my P4, I thought other members might like to hear how I tackled the job. I might add that I was a little apprehensive of doing this myself, but following warm encouragement from Adrian, the Ilford TC, I had a go.

To ease removal of offending nuts and bolts, these were sprayed generously with releasing oil - WD40 or Plus Gas.

Jack up one side of the car under the front coil spring, preferably with a heavy duty jack, sufficiently to take off all the spring pressure, which then allows full removal of the two plates which make up the top link of the suspension. For safety's sake support the car elsewhere in addition. I used an axle stand under the radius arm.

Having removed the hub cap and wheel, loosen the innermost nuts securing the bolt which passes through the bushes for the mounting of link to chassis. Then do likewise with the nuts for the outer mounting of link to kingpin.

Separate the bushes from the bolts before trying to extract the two bolts. To do so the link must be completely removed, which requires that the two plates making up the link must be separated. This is done by loosening the four nuts that hold on the plate which carries the rubber rebound bump stop. Having so done the two bolts can be extracted and the two spacers removed. The bump stop plate can now be removed and the link plates will be free to be taken off. Now the suspension bushes can be prised from the inner and outer mountings, first one of each pair, then the other carrying the bolt (pin) with it. Clean all parts, including the mountings in which the bushes go. To replace the bushes and re-assemble is simply a reverse of the dismantling technique. Do not use oil or grease anywhere near the bushes themselves as this hastens their breakdown. *(What about rubber grease? – Ed)* Make sure all the nuts and bolts are well tightened and check again that they are tight after a few hours on the road once the new bushes have settled in.

Peter Rickinson writes: From my own observations of doing this job there are some points which I'd like to add:

1. Watch out that you don't stretch the flexible brake hose, which can easily happen when the brake disc and caliper pivot outwards once the top wishbone has been removed.

2. The hole through which the bushes go, on top of the kingpin assembly, can be quite rusty and, rather than forcing the new bushes in, all slavering in grease, it's quite easy to take a round section file and clean the said hole out - then the bushes fit.
3. Waxoyl is an excellent lubricant for these parts.
4. The original bushes are available. I didn't get them or the Metalastik A60 substitute. I used BL Mini rear sub-frame lower trunion bushes. These are the correct diameter but rather shorter than the originals and of softer rubber. I doubt they'll last but they only cost me 11p each...

Mini engine stabilizer bushes will not fit.

Peter Rickinson   *January 1979*

PETROL PIPES

As petrol pipe corrosion appears to be a common occurrence on P4s, I thought other members might like to hear how I tackled the problem on my 1956 '75'.

On my car the length of pipe over the rear axle was so rusty it just crumbled to pieces. However, the section from the centre cross-member up into the engine compartment was coated with oil and hence well preserved. I decided to re-new from the centre cross-member to the union in the rear wheel-arch.

The materials required are galvanised steel tube ($\frac{5}{16}$ ins o.d.) and some form of coupler to make the joins. It so happens that $\frac{5}{16}$ equals 7.94mm and so 8mm compression-type couplers, as used for micro-bore central heating, are ideal. The pipe I obtained from a motor-factor at £1.48 for 10 feet and the couplers from a builders' merchants at 35p each.

The tube is quite easily bent by hand pressure as the curves involved are not too acute. The most difficult curves to form are those adjacent to the elbow in the rear wheel-arch, as there are three bends close together. Removing the old pipe is no problem. Undo the securing clips where possible. It is not possible to reach the screws holding some of the clips, so these must be prised open to release the pipe. The pipe is then cut with a junior hacksaw and the rear section removed.

Using the original as a pattern, form the three bends at the extreme rear end. Work inwards from the end – it is easier to grip the pipe if you allow a bit extra beyond the first bend which can be cut off later. Form the curve to follow the chassis over the rear axle and then cut off enough pipe to reach about as far as the battery box. Working from the wheel-arch it is possible to thread the pipe between the chassis and the body. It may be necessary to bend the flange on the body outwards slightly to give clearance. When the pipe is in place it can be bent upwards to follow the line of the chassis. This process is actually harder to describe than it is to do. Of course, if you take the body off there would be no problem!

Trim off the extra pipe and connect up to the elbow (preferably with a new olive). Fit the pipe into the clips, positioning it by a bit of judicious bending. Now measure up the almost straight length to join the existing pipe to the new rear section. Join up with the couplers, re-fit the remaining clips and check that the pipe is not strained or rubbing anywhere.

You can now sit back and forget the problem for another 22 years or so – and think of all the petrol you'll be saving.

David Messenger   ***January 1979***

FAN MODIFICATION

In recent issues of Overdrive there have been suggestions to remove the fan for quicker warm up and economy. The pros and cons were discussed in brief. The following compromise has proved satisfactory even in heavy traffic.

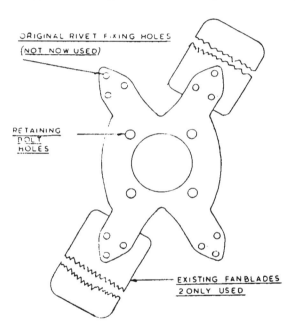

ORIGINAL RIVET FIXING HOLES
(NOT NOW USED)

RETAINING
BOLT
HOLES

EXISTING FAN BLADES
2 ONLY USED

There are four blades on the fan hub, each held in place by three rivets. If one side of the rivets is drilled to the surface of the centre web and then punched through, the blade will come away from the assembly. If this is repeated on the opposite side the result is a two-bladed fan with reasonable balance, capable of keeping the engine cool in heavy traffic.

January 1979

REAR HUB OIL SEALS

It seems to be a widely held view that special equipment is required to remove rear hub oil-seals on P4's.

The Autobook manual states that special tools are needed to service both bearing and oil-seal. This is not the case. The Rover manual is also not clear on this point.

The Rover tool No. 275870 is only required to separate the whole assembly. If everything else is in good order, the seal only may be changed quite simply.

Reference to Fig. E-3 (Rover Manual) shows that the seal is pressed into a sleeve in the housing and contacts the bearing securing sleeve. With the assembly removed from the axle it is simply a matter of pulling out the seal.

"How?" you cry.

The following tip was given to me many years ago by an old Rover storeman.

Drill 2 or 4 equally spaced holes in the outside metal part of the seal. Insert self-tapping screws (NOT countersunk head) into the holes. Take great care to avoid damage. Lever under, or pull on, the screw heads and the seal may be fairly readily extracted.

The new seal can be gently tapped into place with a hammer and drift.

The seal is an ordinary 2¾" x 1⅞" x ½" seal and is easily obtained from a bearing/seal specialist.

I have carried out this job on a number of cars with complete success. Failure of these seals seems to be a common problem, so I don't think that fitting a second-hand unit would be worth all the extra work involved – only to risk another seal failure in the near future.

David Messenger   *April 1979*

EVEN A ROVER SOMETIMES WILL NOT START!

It can happen to the best of us at times, and it happens to some more often than it should!

Firstly, no matter how highly we respect our cars this is no time for emotion; we must apply logic. The stories we have all heard about certain cars being "bad starters" does not apply to the P4. If everything is working as Solihull intended then the car will start on the button.

I will divide this article into two parts: the first looking at the problem of a car that refuses to start after being parked for some time, and second, the roadside breakdown and its primary causes.

If the car refuses to start when it has previously behaved perfectly, it is nobody's fault. On the other hand, if you are aware that the battery won't hold its charge, or the H.T. leads leak and track at the slightest hint of dampness, you cannot really blame anyone but yourself when one cold, wet morning your are late for work and the "longship" refuses to move. However, Guild members are sympathetic types and even though it may serve you right, let us look at the problem and try to get you on the road again.

When you turn the key or press the starter and the engine doesn't start one of three things must happen: the engine will spin over on the starter but not fire, it won't turn over at all, or it turns over so slowly as to make no difference. If the last is the case, the cause is most likely to be a weak battery and then you will be glad you chose a P4 as the starting handle will probably get you running. Poor connections, either live or earth, may show similar symptoms but they are more likely to produce no reaction from the starter at all, as will a very flat battery. Switch on the headlamps - if they only glow dimly you have a purely electrical fault. If the lights are bright the most likely cause is the starter motor or solenoid.

If the engine spins over but shows no sign of firing (unless you have flooded it, in which case there will be a strong smell of petrol under the bonnet or at the exhaust pipe) your problem is either: no/insufficient sparks or lack of fuel in the cylinders.

The most common cause of breakdown is ignition trouble but with a P4, with the exception of the '80', switching on the ignition and listening for the click of the petrol pump is advised. A sharp tap on the casing will often persuaded a sticking pump to resume service.

Checking for a spark is the next thing to do. Remove a plug lead, expose its metal end and hold it close to the cylinder head whilst pressing the solenoid button, or on later models, getting someone to crank the engine for you (ignition switched on, of course). You should get a sharp, visible and audible spark jumping across the gap. If you do, remove the plugs and check them. If you don't, take your check back a stage. Disconnect the coil H.T. lead from the top of the distributor, hold it close to a good earth, take the distributor cap off and with ignition on, flick the contact breaker points. A very healthy spark (or a belt up your arm) confirms that all is well on the H.T. side upstream of the distributor cap and the low tension side is obviously doing its job well. The problem is now likely to be distributor cap, rotor arm or H.T. leads. It may only be dampness. Remember to check the cap centre contact and look for signs of a hairline crack running from a pickup contact inside the distributor cap. If there is no spark or only a weak one from the coil, then look at the low tension wiring. Start by cleaning the contact breaker points. Ensure everything is dry - a squirt of WD40 or similar. Check the low tension lead from distributor body to coil for breaks and tracking. If all is well in the low tension department you must suspect the coil or ignition switch. Check that the high tension lead is making good contact at the coil. Without any test instruments the only way of telling is substitution of coil or switch with units you know to be good.

Should everything be working correctly on the ignition circuit then lack of fuel to the cylinder must be checked. Check the fuel gauge – don't laugh, most of us do it at least once! Next, disconnect fuel pipe from the carburettor and switch on ignition ('80' owners crank engine). A regular pulse of fuel should come out – please be careful, it is dangerous stuff. Slackening the union and holding a rag round the joint is safer on a hot engine. If the fuel does not appear and there is fuel in the tank, your problem is either faulty pump (replace or repair) or blocked fuel line (clear by blowing or use a foot pump). If fuel is reaching the carburettor, check that the needle isn't stuck by pressing the plunger on S.U. body (sorry '80' owners, you also have a different carburettor) then remove the air cleaner and peer down the venturi to see if fuel is appearing whilst cranking the engine. Make sure that the dashpot lifts and falls freely and that the needle has not dropped – it has been known. '80' owners check for blocked jets.

By now you should be underway again so let us look at the causes of roadside breakdowns. These also invariably take place when it is raining, you are late and miles from the nearest garage or telephone. It would be very handy to be able to fix the trouble on the spot. I am sure we all have ideas about spares to carry and this is obviously a personal matter which each individual resolves in his own way. I once took so many tools and spares, including a battery operated arc-welder, on a camping holiday to Cornwall that the boot would not accommodate the water carriers, sleeping bags and football. The complaints from the children, squashed in the back seat, convinced me that I must compile a list of essentials.

Fan Belt: make sure it is the correct one by fitting the new one and carrying the old one as a spare. I have never used one but I believe that an emergency belt can be a quick, clean answer which does not require tools or the need to get filthy; but fit the proper belt later.

Points: are the most common causes of breakdown. You will also need feeler gauges to set the gap, but a visiting card can be used – and it works.

Spark Plug: not that nasty old one on the garage bench, treat yourself to a new one!

Condenser: perhaps a rare cause of breakdown but cheap and small to carry.

Hoses: even if you call expert help it is doubtful that they will carry P4 hoses. Ideally, replace with new and carry old, sound ones for spares.

Wire: a coil of wire can solve so many problems from electrics to supporting a loose exhaust system.

Tools: I carry too many and will probably continue to do so, but bare essentials are: Phillips and ordinary screwdriver, small electrical screwdriver, pair of pliers and, although I hate them, an adjustable spanner has its uses. If you are fortunate enough to have a complete tool tray under the dash so much the better. Also a can of WD40, or similar, for damp electrics and a roll of PVC electrical tape.

Workshop Manual: essential for data.

Now to the car. You have no doubt sworn and tried vainly to restart it. Switch on the ignition, check petrol gauge and water temperature. It may be the wrong time to mention it, but on later models the dual fuel pump may have stuck through lack of use. Occasional use of reserve – just to keep it free – is a worthwhile dodge, at least you will know for the next time you need reserve. Water troubles are a common cause of breakdown. If the temperature gauge reads high, carefully lift the bonnet and allow the radiator to cool before removing the cap with a rag over the top. I recently saw a girl covered in boiling water and steam on a garage forecourt – she learnt the hard and painful way! Check for split hoses, leaking radiator and loose or broken fan belt. If there is no obvious water loss then suspect the thermostat. Remove it, you will do no harm without it, warming up will simply be much slower.

If the gauges are reading normal then it is worth a glance at the electrical connections – has a battery lead worked loose? Are the ignition connections loose? Especially the Lucar terminals as used on the coil. If you have driven through rain or surface water, are the electrics damp? –WD40 to the rescue!

Spark plugs are unlikely to cause a complete breakdown. One plug may break down – even two – but this would become obvious when driving. My personal choice is N.G.K. plugs. My '110' can eat Champions in 2,000 miles. But I am sure other people would have their own favourite.

If you are still unable to start, then go through the previous steps of checking ignition system and fuel supply, but bear in mind that a faulty starter motor or solenoid will not cause a breakdown. And especially for '80' owners, a blocked jet will rarely cause a total breakdown – usually a large flat spot or loss of power.

By now 90% of you should be under way, the other 10% are looking worried, reaching for the workshop manual or calling the local garage. Your problem is more difficult to diagnose and may need garage equipment to locate the problem. Just one last item I have met twice myself on late model cars. The driving dog on the base of the distributor can work loose and completely disrupt the ignition timing. An infuriating problem as you have plenty of sparks but they are coming at the wrong time, Symptoms usually include back-firing and explosions in the carburettor.

I have compiled a flow chart which should quickly locate the cause of breakdown in most cases, and I suggest keeping a copy of it in the car. Even if you feel competent to deal with a breakdown it is useful to follow a logical step by step guide, if only to reduce the anxiety level. I don't like to admit it but I have stripped down a carburettor only to find I had run out of petrol!! You may find that you have diagnosed the problem but require a spare which is unobtainable at the local garage. This is the time to contact one of the P4 Breakdown Rescue Volunteers who may well have the spare part or be able to locate it quickly.

Best wishes and may you only need to test your breakdown skills on your neighbour's car.

Kevin Bentley   *May 1980*

REVERSING ELECTRICS TO NEGATIVE EARTH

Most owners will not wish to do this, but I play with ham radio and wanted to maintain a morning contact with a station in New Zealand on my way to work. Modern amateur radio gear is quite capable of being used mobile without much worry over the battery coping, but it is all negative earth. The same goes for all cassette players and combined radio-cassettes that are generally available in dual polarity. Old valve radios can be converted from positive to negative earth with a little time and effort.

This is the sequence of operations:

Disconnect the battery and remove it.

Obtain and fit clamp-type battery leads that enable the old leads of restricted length to be extended so that negative can go to positive, and vice versa.

Disconnect the clock and any radio or cassette equipment.

Check the condition of the armoured lead that goes up to the front of the car along the chassis. Repair and insulate, or replace, as necessary.

Bring the battery to the front of the car, and disconnect the dynamo leads. Connect a stout wire between car body (earth) and the negative dynamo connection. Take another stout wire, connect to the positive terminal of the battery, and flash it across the "F" terminal on the dynamo - do not hold the wire on. This procedure serves to repolarise the dynamo coils.

Re-connect the battery with the new reversed leads, and reconnect the dynamo as before.

Start up to check that all works, and that the charging circuit is operational. Of course, the ammeter will show a _discharge_ when charging, and a charge when discharging.

The battery box cover, and a prominent under bonnet position, e.g. the cross member in front of the radiator, should be clearly marked to the effect that "This vehicle is negative earth". One day the services of the AA, RAC or a garage may be required......

In-car entertainments can now be reconnected appropriately, carefully checking the polarity.

The clock poses a problem, as its polarity cannot be changed. The case serves as the earth for the clock lamp, so I decided to dispense with it. The case was then wrapped in several layers of old-fashioned cloth insulating tape, then taking the lead that used to go to the insulated terminal to the earth, and the old earth lead to the insulated terminal. The clock can be refitted and will be securely held by the insulating tape, and is then started in the normal way.

The SW & CB (or + and -) connections of the coil can be reversed, but this may adversely affect the amount of ignition interference heard over the radio. Use whichever suits your circumstances.

Peter Rickinson   _September 1980_

INTERIOR RENOVATION

In previous issues of Overdrive there have been several references to renovation of window frames but little has been said of glove-box lids, corner filler sections and the all wood fascia rails on pre 1959 models.

I have restored completely these parts on my 1954 '60' and the results are excellent.

To start with glove-box lids; I had considered (briefly) doing them in-situ but thought better of it. To remove the lid from hinges it is necessary to unscrew the hinges from the wood of the lid itself. It is impossible to remove the hinges from the lower fascia rail without removing the entire rail. Hinges are concealed under the leathercloth covering to the rear of the lids. The covering is attached at an awkward angle by small tacks which have to be prised out with a sharp screwdriver. Often the heads break off which makes removal of cloth easy but leaves the pins in the wood. Hinges are then unscrewed and it is then easy to extricate the lid from the check strap on the left by sliding the arm to the forward end of the slot where there is an enlarged 'eye' for this purpose.

To remove the corner fillers there is one self tapping screw at the top and a nut behind the stainless steel rail. Take care not to score the veneer on this piece as you slide it down behind the rail.

Working on parts indoors makes the whole thing much easier. Take off all components taking care not to damage any of the wood. The clip for the lid and the runner for the check strap are prone to rust so emery off all traces and coat with clear polyurethane to prevent further corrosion. Take care removing the leather-cloth which is stiffened internally with damp-proof card. I used a smooth knife to gently lever the tacks out of the wood. You may have to replace the thin strips of card that go round the edges as they are usually in pieces when revealed. It's all straight forward if you are careful and use suitable tools for the job.

I used paintstripper to remove varnish from the bare lid. When it's all been removed using a flat bladed knife, wash the surface thoroughly using a sponge. Avoid immersing completely in water in case the wood warps. Allow to dry and then sand to remove all traces of old varnish. Use sandpaper in the direction of grain and finish with the finest paper. Then wipe over with methylated spirits - twice, to make sure it really is clean. Allow to dry, then mix up clear polyurethane 50/50 with white spirit or thinners (N.B. clear polyurethane seems to produce a good colour and brings out the natural grain really well). It is obviously unnecessary to coat the wood under the leather-cloth section so the lid can be rested on this between coats. Allow 6 hours between coats and very lightly sand over the surface with flour paper and then wipe with meths between each coat. Six or seven coats gives a good surface and does not hide the texture and grain. After the final coat, allow to dry under a cover a few inches above the lid so that there is little chance for dust to settle. Leave to dry hard for 24 hours and then for a really good finish wipe gently with T-Cut in the direction of the grain. This will remove any bits on the surface and leave it very smooth. Wipe clean and polish with a wax furniture polish.

Replace all components noting the following:

1. Some leathercloth bits need glueing - use Bostik or UHU and clean the cloth whilst removed with soap and water.
2. To retack the leathercloth (with thin card inserts) use the old tack holes where possible - new tacks where necessary and use a block of wood between hammer and cloth to prevent damage.
3. Don't forget to attach the check strap before the hinges.
4. The leathercloth has to be left unfastened at the back until the hinges are fixed. Then place a screwdriver on each tack and hammer on the screwdriver carefully pulling the lining taut as you do so. It is otherwise impossible to get at the tacks with a hammer.

The 6 coats operation applies to all the wood. I did the fascia rail in-situ and produced good results, but apparently it is easy to remove. And don't forget the tool tray.

Now it is all replaced it looks perfect which is more than I can say about the rest of the interior but - one thing at a time.

Matt White   *May 1981*

GUDGEON PIN REMOVAL - '60', '75', '90' AND '105' MODELS

To remove the piston and con-rod assemblies of all models (barring the '80', '95', '100' and '110' series) It is necessary to extract their gudgeon pins. Typically these are a relatively loose fit and the job gives every appearance of being straightforward. However, a snag arises by virtue of the sloping engine block face greatly restricting your ability to drift out the pins from above via the combustion chambers, the workshop manual specifies the need for a special extracting tool.

An easy DIY method which reduces the risk of damaging the pistons and con-rod bushes is as follows:

1. Unbolt and remove the exhaust manifold. (You have to do this for a proper decoke anyway.)
2. Extract the exhaust valves.
3. Unbolt the big-ends and push the pistons up their bores. (Note that by having earlier removed the exhaust valves you run no risk of inadvertently scoring a piston on a protruding, open exhaust valve.)
4. Remove both circlips from each piston assembly.
5. Cut a length of ½" wooden dowel (about 12" is fine). Pass one end through the exhaust port of the cylinder concerned until it butts against the gudgeon pin. Gently drift out the pin.

Added advantages of this method are that the con-rod remains supported once the pin is out (no nasty clang as it drops onto those beautiful journal surfaces - which you should have bound with masking tape by now anyway!) and a fine degree of control can be exercised.

Keith Coman   *January 1982*

THE P4 BOOT LOCK

The boot handle/lock like the door handles of a P4 is Mazak and prone to severe pitting. If a replacement boot lock is obtained from a breakers yard the first problem is likely to be obtaining the appropriate key. The '95' and '110' models carry the key identification on the serial number plate at the nearside front door, but in any event the lock number is stamped on the steel latch operating bar '8' in the diagram. However, whilst the lock number is shown the series. (FA, FP etc.) is not, but can be determined by trial and error as only a key of the appropriate series will readily enter the lock.

Having obtained a suitable key you may be home and dry. On the other hand you may find that despite liberal doses of penetrating oil it won't budge and dismantling is the only solution.

The same procedure applies whether the lock is seized in the locked or unlocked position. With the assembly the right way up, use a ¹⁄₁₆" drift to drive the pin 1 downwards. The fulcrum tube 2 can then be driven out from right to left. Separate the handle from the mounting bracket 3 to reveal the lock cylinder retaining pin 4 which again can be driven out forcing it from right to left. Do not be tempted to use any force to move the locking bolt 6 at this stage. Inject some penetrating oil into the hole left by the removal of 4, take the handle by one of its ears and swing smartly down onto a soft wooden block so that the point of impact is close to but not on the lock cylinder 5. With luck the lock cylinder will drop out.

If this fails, drive out the dowel 7 and remove the latch operating bar 8. Carefully drill a ¹⁄₁₆" hole tight against the locking bolt as in fig. 3 and pass a fine drift (or a blunted panel pin) down the hole and using gentle taps force the lock cylinder out. (If you have a ¹⁄₁₆ long drill you could drill a deeper hole aiming for the shoulder on the lock cylinder.) Having removed the lock cylinder the locking bolt can be safely removed.

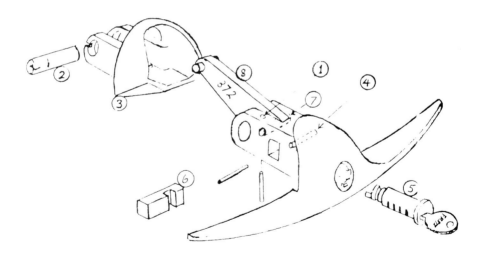

Clean, lubricate and reassemble using either the original locking cylinder or the one from your discarded handle so that the key fits both boot and glove box as it should. Of course an easier way to achieve this might be to remove boot handle and glove box lock from the same vehicle in the breaker's yard.

E.Bromwell   *May 1982*

HOW IS YOUR AUNTIE?

We often find ourselves owning a P4 rather late in the normal car lifespan, and intend to take the car as a regular means of transport rather than to only use the car in fine weather. So we have a late start but doubtless hopes of much pleasurable Rover motoring ahead.

Few P4's, I would think, are bought still with sound coats of paint beneath the car where protection is really needed. On my two P4's, which I take as typical, 100,000 miles plus and 23 and 24 years old, there is quite a considerable amount of original protection now missing. There is surface rust on the underbody and chassis, and from time to time rust has damaged small areas on both body and chassis. Welded new plate repairs have been necessary.

To be realistic we live in a country which is often damp and I doubt that at one time I will have repaired all that needs attention in a given area beneath, have all cleaned thoroughly, degreased then primed and painted with an ideal protective finish. In short, waxoyl or similar, thinned oil, sprayed and brushed is going to be the protection applied and repeated. This is more than either car has had before with previous owners.

Road dirt is scraped and brushed off, paying particular attention to dirt that has built-up in corners, top surfaces and around pipes and fixings (taking care not to cause extra repair work). It is a Forth Bridge type of job if the car is used in all weathers, but done in sections, combined with other jobs it is not too bad. If time is short then an oil spray at the local garage would be better than no action at all being taken.

During a break in the Winter weather or/and at Winter's end, when road salt usage ceases, a garden hose can be used beneath Auntie's wings, paying particular attention to areas around lamps, flange joints and the brake servo reservoir tank. If the car is raised slightly, even one side at a time, the jet can be used to clean quite an amount of the chassis. Whether you wish to flush out the chassis cross-members is up to individual choice; I do, but go for a drive with right and left hand curves afterwards to clear out the water from the drain holes. Two cautions, do not wet too close to engine and take care not to direct jet on front suspension top link housings just cover coil springs - the holes in chassis top will allow suspension bump stop cones beneath to fill. They unfortunately have no drain holes. This is likely the reason for their rusting and eventually collapse.

Existing protective paint and underseal which is removed during cleaning or by the oil/waxoyl used is usually that which is fairly frail.

So far it has been general and there may be members who can speak well of steam cleaning then protection etc.

There are positions on Auntie's chassis where rust can easily get a hold. Mainly the problems stem from a wetted build-up of road dirt. Views extracted from the Rover Parts Catalogue have been used, with certain extras blanked out, to avoid lengthy descriptions of areas I have found in need of attention.

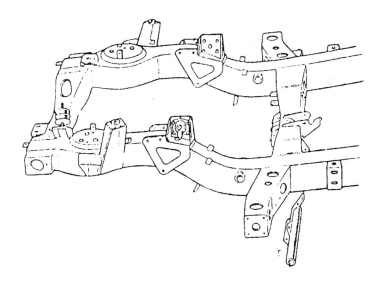

1. **Front Suspension Rebound Stop/Damper Bracket.**
   In this area, hidden to some extent by Inner Wing Panels and Suspension Top Links, road dirt builds on the Rebound Stop and the top surface of the chassis against the Damper Bracket (which doubles as a brake hose mounting). Rust here attacks the chassis and particularly the damper bracket, which on a few cars has been known to partly sever from chassis. This dirt should be cleaned off and waxoyl applied generously.

2. **Steering Idler Mounting (L.H. Side of P4)**
   Steering Box Mounting (R.H. Side of P4)
   The chassis mounting arrangement for above is such that two bolts with distance tubes pass over and close to the chassis. Dirt fills the

space between the bolts, on the chassis top, particularly on the side mounting the idler. Dirt also builds up in the adjacent spaces inside the body mounting brackets and can be seen from beneath the front wings. This dirt if not regularly cleaned out will cause rusting, when wetted, of the chassis. If this cannot be done when dirt is seen, then dribble oil into the dirt, but clean out at a later time.

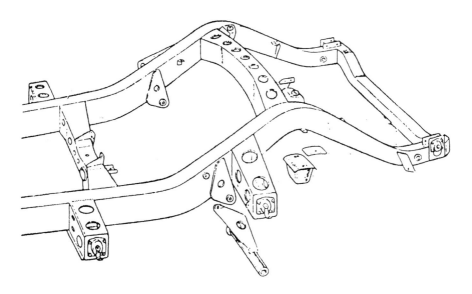

Unfortunately water is to some extent allowed to run from the drainage channels on the top of the front wings diagonally down the bulkhead mountings for inner wings (or wheel arches) and so on to the chassis. Whether this is design or fault on my car I am not sure - any comments?

3.   **Attachments to Chassis**
Rear Axle Bump Stops and Packers, Jacking Brackets and items bolted in position and exposed to wetness are disadvantaged unless a sealant is used to prevent ingress of water between the item and chassis (or body). Normally water can remain for long periods to rust the metal; the rust flake expands and thus progressively enlarges the gap, damaging the two metals (distortion can often be seen).

become saturated and water will proceed further into the door. Thus after 20-30 years they can benefit from renewal since the aluminium part becomes fragile and may crack whilst the felt-fur casing becomes worn and rotten. At worst they may break off and get entangled in the window regulator. Replacement draught strip is available in 2 metre lengths and costs £2.30. Whilst removing the outer length be careful to salvage as many of the securing clips as possible since they are in short supply. The inner strips are riveted to a support and the more substantial rivets on the earlier cars ('55) and more likely to crack upon removal than the more pliable later rivets ('63) which may be used again – although alternatives here could be a little easier. It is possible to replace the draught strips by removing the window mouldings whilst the window glass remains in-situ.

The felt around the flexible glass channelling around the top of the window may also benefit from removal and like the draught strips replacement roll is available.

Meanwhile the window regulators then get a good dousing... this not only controls the rivets making their action difficult but in extreme cases can rot the lifting channel for the glass so the rust accumulated expels the glazing strip and the glass together; this can provide endless hours of fun and entertainment at the wrong time.....

On our wedding day ten years ago the chauffeur desired more fresh air, and got it, as the drivers door glass crashed down into the door. Not wishing to face a draughty 90 mile trip home the groom was seen, later in the day, fishing around discreetly in the door, taking some corrective action. (One day in my life when overalls were not thought necessary – just goes to show...)

All this because of excessive corrosion caused by the ingress of excess water. Later cars, I note, have galvanised parts for the window support channels.

The solution was to fit (after painting the relevant parts with waxoyl) user replacement regulators and a window glass complete with lifting channel from a later car. Certain self-tapping screws can be very difficult to shift – so take care that the screwdriver doesn't slip and damage the softer aluminium panels.

The correct position for the support channels to ensure free window regulation can take hours of fiddling...

After all is reassembled a good spray of waxoyl all around the inside of the door is desirable – this prevents further corrosion (yes even on the aluminium) but has some lubricating properties as well. Where does the water go after that? Ask the owner of any late '95'/'110'! This lack of drainage ensures that the door casings (internal) get damp and may even rot considerably – even alloy doors may corrode just above (and mostly behind) the stainless door mouldings; sufficiently to lift the paint anyway, It is therefore better to keep owners manuals and maps in the glove pocket to prevent the hinges staining the paper, and a screwed up cloth propping the mouth of the map pocket open will speed up the drying out. Should your door casing look 'tired' and 'shabby' yet not too moth-eaten then try giving them a good scrub and wash the carpets thoroughly at the bottom. (Try Fairy Liquid and a soft scrubbing brush). This can have very good results – perhaps raising the state of the door trim – after all, before you became the owner of your P4 how many previous owners would have bothered to give the car a decent spring clean?

This approach also avoids the necessity of buying new carpets, leather upholstery and headlining materials to match newly (unoriginal) retrimmed doors!

November 1983

Paul Hart

BONNET RELEASE

With his renewal, Mr Bricket from Fareham, Hants asked about the problem of releasing the bonnet when the inner cable has parted company with the release lever. The workshop manual states:

"Care should be taken that the inner cable is fixed securely to the arm on the bonnet catch plate before shutting the bonnet as it will be found impossible to open the lid other than by operating the cable".

Despite the above warning, Rover designers did not expect the luckless owner to have the ability of Paul Daniels. Instead they thoughtfully provided a small round hole in the grille top support, through which, with the aid of a screwdriver or similar tool the bonnet release lever could be operated.

The hole is to be found immediately to the left of the grille badge, high up behind the grille bars.

Whilst you still have the luxury of a working bonnet release, it will help to raise the bonnet and familiarise yourself with this simple operation. So who needs Paul Daniels? Well sometimes.

Colin Blowers

January 1984

REAR AXLE BREATHER

To prevent pressure building up in the rear axle, a breather valve is fitted to the top of the casing, usually on the offside, although some models may have one valve on each side. If the valve should become blocked or stuck for any reason then pressure that should be allowed to escape into the atmosphere is restricted within the axle and eventually seeks a way out. This condition may cause oil leakage at the seals with possible contamination of brake linings.

Removal and checking of the valve takes only a few minutes with the rear road wheels removed. (Use axle stands for safety)

Firstly clean around the valve housing to prevent any dirt or grit from entering the axle casing and, using a suitable spanner unscrew the valve. Older pattern breathers have a hole in the side of the housing whilst later types are fitted with a shroud.

Clean the outside of the breather and gently shake, the ball inside should be heard to move. Blowing through the bottom screwed opening should be possible with little resistance, if however the ball is stuck on its seating a wash in petrol should free it. This simple task may save your rear brake linings from contamination but will of course not cure leaks from defective oil seals.

Colin Blowers

March 1984

FRONT SUSPENSION OVERHAUL

What forced me into such a major undertaking was the discovery, during a routine check, that the R/H road spring had broken what amounted to a turn and a half off the bottom. The broken piece was jammed against the spring support plate and the actual break was quite rusty. So it must have been fractured for some time. I've no idea when it happened as there was no noticeable change in the handling of the car. (The handling was, I must admit, not good!) I had noticed the tyres wearing unevenly but I thought that this was due to worn top link bushes. It probably was but I should think a broken spring didn't help matters. The car did not lean over particularly either.

It took me about fifteen minutes to decide to go the whole hog and dismantle everything except the swivels. (I think that when they need doing I'll let someone else do those!) With the aid of a friend I set about the task. I had soaked all the nuts and bolts the previous day with WD40 and again before I started.

The first job was to jack the car up sufficiently to allow the springs to drop. I placed 12" axle stands under the chassis on both sides where the front outriggers emerge.

The shock absorbers and torsion rod pins must be disconnected from the bottom support plate at this stage. Luckily the shock absorbers simply sheered their bottom bolts very easily. (Note: Add two shock absorbers to the shopping list!) Also remove the central jacking plate.

A trolley jack, by the way, is essential for this job but you don't need a block as described in the manual. I jacked up one side immediately under the bottom spring support plate until the car started to rise as well as the suspension – I knew the spring was then fully compressed. I removed the 'L' section straps on top of the bottom links and slowly undid the nuts securing the bottom plate a little at a time. Eventually a gap appeared between the plate and the bottom links and as I continued the gap became larger but stopped at about ½". Then gingerly I removed all the nuts and bolts leaving two central ones till last. With these out the only thing holding the spring up is the jack and standing well back I used its lowering control from as far away as I could get. Springs are after all a bit lethal if unleashed suddenly! Very slowly the jack lowered and the spring extended and dropped out of the chassis followed by the cone for the bump rubber. I could just remove the jack from under the released spring and manoeuvre the spring and all its assembly out and away from the car. (I think 12" axle stands are the minimum) All this was repeated for the other side and then an inspection of all components. The offending spring was broken in two places. The cones for the bump rubbers were almost rusted through – I could crush the ends with my fingers! The "spring support plate, inner" was non-existent on one side and wafer thin on the other. The holes where the shock absorbers fit were so elongated that they were twice as long as they were wide and the big nut underneath the support assembly was corroded solidly in place. The bottom links came off easily enough and were in good condition, but I could only get one pin out of four free. The top links were O.K. and replacement of the rubber bushes here is quite straightforward with the road spring removed. With it in place it is essential to jack up the wheel till the gap between top links and the bump stop is at its maximum. The radius-arm balls are also easy except that the nuts are difficult to get a spanner to on top of the housing.

Before reassembly of the suspension I had to amass a huge pile of new and second-hand parts. The cones for the bump rubbers had to be partly rebuilt in welded metal (thicker steel than the original was used). This cone is not a precision part and as long as the dimensions are similar to the original there should be no problems. Re-fixing of the rubber to this calls for some invention if new parts are not available. I bonded them in place with epoxy-resin – seems to work as well. In fact the suspension is hardly ever stressed to the point that it will contact its bump stop. I also needed two "spring support plates, inner", two bottom support plates – which incorporate the holes for shock absorber and torsion rod fixings, two rebound rubbers for the top links, two self locking nuts for bottom bump stops, two torsion rod link pins (the replacements were in stainless steel), two shock absorbers and twenty rubber bushes – quite a pile!

Before putting all this lot back every part was cleaned and if necessary painted. Waxoyl is good for every part of the suspension. Rubber bushes and for that matter everything (including the mechanic) was covered before reassembly.

Replacement is straightforward – after replacing the top links the bottom links can go on before the spring is inserted. The cone with bump rubber, the spring and support bush and the bottom support plate have to be manhandled on to the trolley jack and into the spring aperture – accurately so that everything lines up and the ten bolt holes are aligned with each other. You may have to make several attempts at this because as you compress the spring to bring the support plate up to the links it becomes impossible to move the assembly laterally – it sounds complicated to describe but it will be obvious when you do it. Do the nuts up evenly and slowly all round until everything is tight. Make quite sure everything is secure before removing the jack. Fitting of shock absorbers and torsion rod is also easy and straightforward.

The bottom link pin nuts, the nuts securing the radius arm ball housing, the top link bushes and the torsion rod chassis bushes must be finally tightened when the car is in normal riding position. The top link ones are almost impossible to do up with the wheels in place so you can duplicate this position with the wheel off by using a trolley jack under the spring. A few tips – a small blowtorch will aid removal of the bottom link pins if they are difficult to remove – the rubber bushes will soften enough to pull the pins out. A nut splitter is invaluable for removing the large nut under the support bush as it leaves the threads in perfect condition. Necessary tools – a trolley jack, axle stands, ¼ BSF, ⅜ BSF ⁵⁄₁₆ and ⁷⁄₁₆ spanners and matching sockets, waxoyl.

The special bolts and locknuts in the front of the radius arms may need adjusting so that the wheels do not foul at full steering lock. Wheel alignment will undoubtedly need adjustment as well.

My car was off the road seven days for the job which actually took four days to complete. Total cost of parts including the re-made cones came to £176 which included about £40 on rubber items alone. I must say it was not a difficult job to accomplish but it did take time and patience and I was quite pleased with myself when I drove for the first time – the change in handling and quietness was amazing! After a week or so driving I did go round and check the nuts and bolts for tightness and found that nearly all could take another quarter of a turn. I had to replace the springs as a pair by the way so that the car sat on an even keel. So there it is – don't be too afraid of attempting something that may look complicated; it might be easier than you think.

Matt White   *May 1984*

OIL FILTER PAPER ELEMENT TYPE

We sell new engines to people who don't change their oil filters – a slogan used in advertisements to make motorists aware of the need to change oil and filters at regular mileages. With little used cars however – and quite a number of P4's fall into this category – the need to change oil and filter becomes necessary at shorter intervals as old oil left in sumps deteriorates and holds harmful acids.

A point worth checking next time you change your oil filter is that the spring and pressure plate are still in-situ at the lower end of the filter bowl. These two items are situated around the centre tube and may sometimes be inadvertently tipped out with the paper filter element. The result is that when the new filter is fitted it simply drops to the bottom of the bowl and performs no useful purpose as oil bypasses the filter to be returned dirty to the sump, rather like having no filter at all. Remember 'We sell new engines...'

Colin Blowers

November 1984

LOOK AFTER YOUR 'SWIVELS'!

Regularly check your swivel or king pins, and after a few months you will be able to diagnose their best maintenance routine. For example, if you have renewed or have had the king pins serviced properly, you should only need check the oil reservoir level say, every three months. This is regardless of mileage, as standing still or moving, they can still deteriorate.

If however, you have little or no knowledge of their condition, I suggest you start on the following programme of investigation:

1. Make yourself a king pin dipstick, either using ⅛ inch steel rod, or brazing rod. If these are not easy to obtain 'borrow' (forever) one of your wife's wire coat hangers. You need a length of about 12 inches and using PVC tape, position a mark 6½ inches from one end.
2. Wire-brush the top of pin and air release bolt head on front side of upper swivel housing and remove both bolts.
3. Check level of oil in pins, it should reach the 6½ inch mark. If it is overfilled, it will escape through the air release hole.

NEVER use a grease nipple in the air release hole as this will only damage the seals. If, incidentally, you find you already have leaky seals, you have two options:

(i) Renew seals – which for the work involved really isn't worth doing without replacing pin and bushes as well.
(ii) Alternatively, cut your losses and make a point of replenishing the oil at regular intervals, say every 5-6 weeks. Providing of course, there is not any noticeable play in the bushes.

If on the first check, you find the oil is very murky, or that someone has unknowingly used grease instead of oil, you will have to remove the bottom cover by undoing the tabs and removing the three set bolts. You can then gently flush out the pin with paraffin.

This may not remove all the grease in the bush oilways, but it will certainly get things moving properly again. Replace bottom cover using some form of gasket sealant, then fill with new oil, allowing time for the oil to trickle from air release hold to find own level. An oil can with a flexible spout is the most useful for this job.

Although 140 grade oil is recommended, 20/50 engine oil is better because being thinner, it has more searching properties. Ideally a 50/50 mixture of Molyslip and multigrade engine oil should be used, although of course, Molyslip is a rather expensive commodity.

So generally speaking, a 2-monthly check should keep your swivels in good lubricated order.

Once the level of oil goes below the 6 inch mark, you will then have, what is known in the trade as 'dry balls' – and we all know how dodgy that can be, so be warned!!

Stan Johnstone   *November 1984*

GET THE BEST FROM YOUR HANDBRAKE! (1953-1964)

Depending on the condition of your handbrake system, i.e. the pawl and ratchet at the driver's end through to the slave cylinders at the rear back plate, only you can decide how much work is needed to bring your handbrake to full efficiency. You may only need to do some of the following jobs to get your brakes working correctly.

The pawl is usually the culprit if the handbrake tends to slip. The ratchet, strangely enough, doesn't seem to wear as much as the pawl. A new pawl is reasonably cheap to buy, and quite simple to fit once you have cleaned all the grit and old grease from the mechanism. A pot of paraffin and a ½" brush is ideal for this. Once clean, you will find you can see exactly how much wear has taken place. Re-grease and replace cover when happy that the pawl is working correctly and that there is not too much side play.

Generally speaking, if the linkage is set to the correct angles, an inefficient handbrake is almost certainly caused by seized wheel cylinders (slaves).That is to say, seized on the brake back plate. To remedy this, jack up the car and support on axle stands. Clamp the rear flexible brake pipe and undo the two metal brake pipes, attached to each wheel cylinder. By clamping the brake pipes, bleeding will only be needed to be done to the rear. Release rods from drawlinks. Remove drums and shoes (noting positions of pull off springs). Unscrew the three self locking nuts from the cylinder (note pull off spring positions) and remove the dust cover plate and slave cylinder from the back plate. If the rubber dust covers are dry and both the pistons are moving freely, retain them in the cylinder with a strong elastic band so that the cylinders can be worked on without the pistons falling out.

If the cylinders show any signs of leaks, they will have to be stripped, and if the bores are not corroded, new seals will have to be fitted. Carefully wire brush the drawlink and tappet channel on the cylinder and the face with the studs. Check bleed screw is workable before replacing, they sometimes seize in the cylinder and are much easier to deal with on the bench. Wirebrush the draw links and tappets and clean rollers. Wirebrush inside and out of back plate around the aperture for the wheel cylinder, smear graphite grease or "copperslip" around both sides of the aperture being careful not to use too much. Fit wheel cylinder and dust cover plate to back plate with spring washers and tighten self locking nuts, (preferably new ones) tighten gradually until the wheel cylinder will just slide up and down in its slots using firm hand pressure on the cylinder.

THIS MOVEMENT IS VITAL, IT DOES IN FACT, PERMIT SELF-CENTRING AND THUS A 'TWO-SHOE' CONTACT.

Replace the shoes having checked that they have plenty of life left. Screw in bleed screw. Fit drawlinks, tappets and rollers with a sparing amount of graphite grease and secure the cover plate firmly to cylinder. Connect brake rod to drawlink and make sure the balance lever is set at the correct angles. One way of doing this is to copy the angles from the workshop manual on to a piece of cardboard with the axle as the datum line. Whilst both the long and short cross-rods are released from the drawlinks it is worth noting that the relay lever is not seized in its bush and also that there is not too much play in the balance lever bush.

Finally, release clamp from rear brake hose and bleed both cylinders. Adjust shoes until they just start to bind and back off adjuster two clicks.

After all this work take the car down the road, check rear view mirror, heave on the 'Shepherd's crook' and you should hear a loud scream from the back tyres.

Whoever said that P4's have got lousy handbrakes!?????

Stan Johnstone   *January 1985*

HOW TO CLEAN YOUR VOKES AIR SILENCER FILTER ELEMENT
(1954-56; '75' & '90' owners)

1) Follow the procedure in the owners manual for cleaning. (Basically removal of the filter element followed by tapping until the dirt drops out; usually grit and fan-lacerated flies etc.) This should be done every 6,000 miles.

2) Replacements are not available, therefore at 18,000 miles the following may help.

   a) Take a modern washing powder and a tall bucket (over half the height of the felt-gauze element) and make up a suitable washing suds solution in the bucket, full of hot water.

   b) "Stonk" the element vigorously up and down in the bucket, holding each end in turn.

   c) When clean, rinse thoroughly in clean tap water to remove all trace of suds. If you are lucky the filter may just fit the kitchen sink.

   d) Peg out to dry. The felt ends may come adrift slightly but a judicious application of Copydex will correct this and James Taylor will never know. The felt may just clean up to Persil whiteness with care. Washing the felt against the direction of the airflow will also help.

3) Refit when dry, or you will have a problem no damp-start will cure!

Paul Hart   *January 1985*

44

TIMING TROUBLE

Has anyone an absolutely infallible method of timing an old, partly worn '110' camshaft fitted to a '100' block with a '100' flywheel? It is obvious that with a '100' flywheel and a '110' camshaft the timing marks and the 'time it on the EP mark' syndrome no longer apply due to the '100' and '110' having their timing EP marks in different places. I've played about with a timing disc and pointer and a dial gauge until I've got dials running round inside of my head and figures with them and a '110' which won't do more than 80 flat out.

The cam has still got its performance if I can find out where it is because the original engine used to go really well. I never experienced any trouble in getting it to the ton and beyond before the motor blew up due to a fracas over big end nuts which those of you who also belong to the R.S.R. will doubtless remember. Those of you who have tried to retime an old camshaft will have found that the exhaust peak will have worn sufficiently to prevent this, mine doesn't have a definite peak any more. The top of the cam on No. 1 wanders about over about 5 degrees at peak. I can hear someone saying 'Why didn't he check the timing with a dial gauge, timing disc and pointer before taking the bloody thing to bits'. No go chaps, the motor seized solid when it went round for the last time. I've at present got it timed up at 12 before on the inlet valve but the engine is still as flat as the proverbial pancake. I've also tried 8 before and 10 before without any juicy results, except that it gollops petrol at 8 before and does about 70. What I've not yet tried is taking out all the cam followers and tappets, and checking these for wear although at 55,000 I would have thought this unnecessary. Having done this I could try taking all the opening and closing times of the valves and their present peaks and see what ideas we can come up with between about a thousand of us. What do you think fellas? And no – I am not going to buy a new camshaft just to time the wretched motor.

March 1985

Reg Varney

GIVE THE ENGINE A TREAT

If you are one of those contented people that believe that if their Rover is running well then 'leave it alone', do not read any further! If on the other hand you like to keep a check on your P4, then the following may, I hope, be useful and interesting advice.

Some of the sad cars I have been invited to do work on have broken my heart on lifting their bonnets. Simply because the Rover is such a reliable car, some owners believe they were serviced for life when they left Solihull. I am a firm believer in regular maintenance and think that if you carry out the following jobs and checks, you will be a much happier driver.

Firstly, regardless of your particular car's annual mileage, a change of oil and filter should be carried out every 3,000 miles. The car should be driven for at least fifteen miles before draining the oil into a suitable bowl, remembering that two gallons is a lot of very hot oil. While this is draining, the filter canister can be removed carefully and after removing the old filter and being careful not to lose the spring and washer inside, the filter holder can be washed out with paraffin. The old rubber sealing ring must be removed. This sometimes can be awkward and difficult and if you are not sure you have removed all of the ring, then it is quicker and safer to remove the whole thing from the engine block, and give it a good clean while you are about it. It is not worth leaving the old seal in, as this can invariably lead to leaks, and is not worth the chance. A small electrician's (or come to that a tall electrician's) screwdriver usually gets it moving though.

With all the old oil removed, replace the drain plug. Incidentally, if it is a little worse for wear, Daniel Young can supply new ones for less than a pound. Well worth it, particularly if the wrong spanner or socket has been used and the flats on the head have become rounded off. I had to remove the sump on Gary Edwards' '100' because the previous owners had mutilated the head of the drain plug so much, nothing would get a grip on it. A long job just for an oil change!

With the new filter firmly in place the new oil can be poured into the engine, remembering on starting up that it will take a while for the oil to get round the engine, so keep the revs down until the green light has extinguished. A safer way is to wind the engine with the starting handle a few turns to prime the system.

Whilst on the messy jobs the oil bath air cleaner (except '110' where a new paper element should be fitted) should be removed and after removing the wire gauze, the bowl should be cleaned and refilled with new engine oil, approx. 1 pint, to the the arrow marked on the side. The gauze should be washed in petrol or paraffin and shaken dry and replaced inside the bowl, which should then be screwed back on to its mounting.

Next a new set of points should be fitted to the distributor and on setting the gap (.015") the ignition timing should be checked. I find that a static check is the most satisfactory way and have found it is more reliable than using a Strobe light. I use a 12 volt inspection light with two crocodile clips but even an old spot light will do the job. Having checked the timing setting for your particular model, attach one lead to the low tension connection on the side of the distributor, and the other to a good earth i.e. engine mounting bolt.

Turn the engine with the crank handle (removing the spark plugs first will facilitate this) until the rotor arm is pointing to No. 1 spark plug, i.e. in a straight line with the engine. With the ignition switched on, turn the handle very slowly until the light just illuminates. Having swivelled back the flywheel cover plate (driver's side on all models except '105R' which is on passenger side), check to see where the firing point is in relation to the pointer on the flywheel cover plate. Usually after just replacing the contact breaker points a small adjustment can be made using the vernier nut on the distributor body. If more adjustment is needed the pinch bolt will have to be slackened on the clamping plate at the base of the distributor and the whole thing rotated slightly until the light comes on at the correct setting on the flywheel. If the light illuminates before the correct mark in degrees has reached the pointer, the timing is too far advanced or conversely if the light comes on after the timing mark, the ignition is retarded.

Adjust until happy that the timing is correct, lock up tightly if clamping plate has been slackened and replace timing cover. Remove leads, replace cap and switch off engine.

While the plugs are removed, it is a convenient time to adjust the exhaust tappets if needed. These should be done with the engine stone cold, whilst the inlets must be adjusted with the engine at full running temperature.

The rule of seven should be employed i.e. With No. 6 valve fully open No. 1 valve should be checked and adjusted as necessary. No. 2 valve should be set with No. 5 valve fully open, and so on. Hence the two valves being checked will always add up to seven.

Time should be taken over tappet settings, as they are vital to the well-being of the engine. If anything, it is better to have slightly bigger gaps than being on the tight side, as too small a gap could result in a burnt valve. When happy with the exhaust tappet settings replace the side cover, preferably with a new gasket.

If the spark plugs haven't done more than 12,000 miles they can be cleaned and regapped to .030 thou. and replaced. Otherwise fit new ones but don't forget to gap correctly before fitting.

The car can then be taken for a good run and returned fully warmed to adjust the inlet valves. Again using the rule of seven.

Finally, the two oil breathers, one on the top rocker box and one on the side rocker cover should be removed and washed in paraffin.

This may all seem a bit basic for the average mechanics amongst us, but I really intended this advice for the 'do-it-yourselfers', who, I am sure, are quite capable of maintaining their own P4's. So just to recap:

Oil change and new filter every 3,000 miles. Points renewed generally speaking every 6,000 miles and plugs, oil bath (paper element on air cleaner of '110' changed every 18,000 miles) and breathers changed or cleaned, respectively every 10-12,000 miles.

March 1985

Stan Johnstone

LOOKED AT YOUR TOP LINKS LATELY?

One of the most hard-working parts of the P4 front suspension is the top link rubber bushes. This is particularly so if the car is run for many miles with old and inefficient shock absorbers. MOT examiners like to get their long and mean levers under the links and charge you the earth to replace the bushes for they know that, basically, it is a straight-forward job to do. So don't be caught out, check yours and if necessary replace them yourself and you will be surprised how simple it is to do.

Tell-tale signs of wear are a ragged edge round the bushes where they are squeezed between the links and the top anchor. Also with the car jacked up at the centre jacking plate, and the wheels removed, a lever can be used between the links and the chassis to determine any excessive movement. If you do decide to tackle this job, make sure that you can obtain the eight new metalastic bushes (4 each side) before starting the work. Not wishing to provoke any panic buying, but Daniel Young was commenting recently that stocks were getting low and that he and our other friends in the spares outlets were negotiating the possibility of re-production of new bushes. However, enough of my intros, let's get on with the job!

Working on one side at a time, jack up the car safely preferably using a trolley jack. Remove wheel and with a bottle jack under the outer end of the bottom links, raise the suspension until the rebound rubber backing plate is 2½ inches away from the chassis extension. This position is also correct for re-assembly and the top link retaining nuts should be finally tightened in this position.

Undo the two ¼ inch BSF bolts securing the rebound rubber plate. Incidentally, the plate is usually all that is there as the rebound rubber is invariably missing, sometime in the late sixties, I would think. Don't worry too much about the absence of these rebound rubbers, as unless you use the M1 a lot they will rarely be needed.

Remove the bolts, distance tubes and plate and loosen the ⅜ inch BSF self-locking nuts on the link pins. The rearward facing nut at the inner end of the top links can be a bit awkward as there isn't much room for movement. If this nut proves to be too stubborn the other 3 nuts and washers can be removed with the front link and rubber and wriggled off, still attached to the link, it can then be removed with the help of a vice. Another problem that can arise is that the metal sleeve inside the metalastic bush (hence the name) can sometimes become rusted to the pin, but with the aid of the vice again and by protecting the thread with the nut screwed back on, it can usually be persuaded to move with a copper faced mallet. If the pins are badly corroded, they will have to be replaced, either with serviceable secondhand ones or new ones, which are still available through the usual channels. Clean the pins thoroughly with a wire brush and emery cloth and smooth out the surface inside the top anchor housing with a half round file.

This preparation is important as it gives a longer life to the new bushes. Before re-assembly, smear Copper slip on to the pins, and bushes. This will not only aid the assembly but will leave a lasting lubricant on the bushes and again lengthen their life.

Systematically tighten the four ⅜ inch nuts and with the 2½ inch gap as described earlier give them a final tighten. Replace the rebound rubber plate, distance tubes and ¼ inch BSF nuts and bolts. Again it must be stressed that the suspension assembly must be raised to give the 2½ inch gap already mentioned. This will ensure that no extra tension or pre-load is put on to the new bushes.

Well, apart from putting the wheel back on and removing the jacks, that's one side done. Not too bad, was it? Much more rewarding and cheaper than letting that MOT garage do it. Generally speaking they are only used to Escorts, Metros and Yugos anyway!

Stan Johnstone

May 1985

COLD START WARNING LIGHT CONTROL

Some P4 owners may have had the same experience as I had when I bought my latest P4. When the cold start knob was pulled out the orange warning light immediately came on, indicating some kind of short in the circuit. Assuming that the fault lay in the cylinder head sender unit, I set about acquiring a replacement from a scrapped P4.

I decided to test the 'new' unit before fitting it and found the same problem existed. I was about to throw it away in frustration when my curiosity got the better of me and I decided to see what the unit contained.

The top plate is made from an aluminium alloy casting and the 'bulb insert' is copper. I separated the two parts with the help of a Stanley knife and revealed a mass of rusted metal within. This was obvious indication of the cause of the problem and also showed that the unit was beyond repair.

I thought that the unit in my own car might be in a similar state but, just in case, I repeated the procedure and found to my delight a perfectly preserved internal assembly. All that had happened was that the locking nut on the outside of the top plate had worked loose and allowed the two parts of the bi-metallic strip unit to rotate so that they were constantly in contact causing the short.

Five minutes with a screw-driver and a suitable sized spanner restored the unit to working condition. I resealed the unit with Araldite and after successfully testing it off the car, refitted it and now have a perfectly working warning light.

The accompanying diagram may help readers to identify the parts referred to in this article.

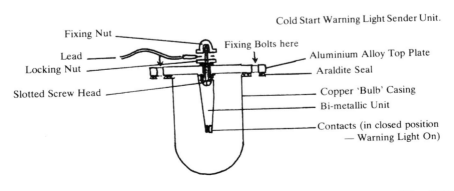

Cold Start Warning Light Sender Unit.

Fixing Nut
Fixing Bolts here
Lead
Aluminium Alloy Top Plate
Locking Nut
Araldite Seal
Slotted Screw Head
Copper 'Bulb' Casing
Bi-metallic Unit
Contacts (in closed position — Warning Light On)

Chris Gough

May 1985

MUDTRAP IDLER

Photo 1

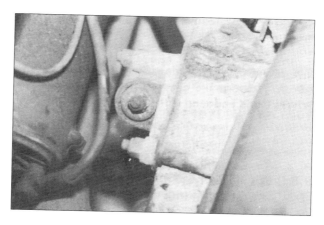

Photo 2

An excellent mudtrap on top of the chassis is the area between the tubular spacers adjacent to the steering idler.

Photo 1 shows a build up of mud to the top of the spacers, with Photo 2 showing what lurked underneath the mud – one large hole which would allow water to enter the chassis causing internal rusting.

Close observation of Photo 2 shows the remains of the sound deadening material which fills parts of the chassis, this acts very much like a sponge retaining water virtually indefinitely once wet.

The photos also show that the idler has been fitted with the modification to the filler plug, i.e. end float adjusting bolt and lock nut, but visual indications are that the idler has not received any lubrication in recent times.

The idler is not shown in most lubrication charts, as in original Rover literature the unit was classed as 'sealed for life', which roughly translated means the life of the oil remaining inside the idler.

Make a rule to top up the idler when topping up the kingpins, SAE 90 being a suitable oil. Remember firstly, before removing the filler plug, to clean around the top of the unit to prevent any road grit from entering. If your idler has the modification, it is advisable to readjust the end float if the filler plug has been removed for oiling purposes.

In this case, before refitting the filler plug, loosen the lock nut and run back the adjusting bolt a few turns, this will prevent the bolt contacting the shaft before the plug is fully tightened.

Replace the filler plug and tighten securely. Using a screwdriver adjust the bolt in a clockwise direction until it contacts the idler shaft, then back off fractionally, this will allow the shaft free movement but will restrict the end float to a minimum. The locknut should then be retightened. Do not be tempted to overtighten the adjusting bolt, this will result in stiff steering and will cause rapid wear to take place on the top idler bush.

On one idler which I recently came across, the lip of the top bush was completely worn away, allowing the collar to rotate against the alloy idler housing, a situation which if left would result in a worn housing. The modification obviously took care of excessive end float, but in this case actually hid a badly worn bush.

Colin Blowers   ***May 1985***

CLUTCH AND BRAKE PEDAL LUBRICATION

Apropos stories to tell, some 5½ years ago, I experienced the brake and clutch pedals acting in concert on my '95'. All attempts at separating them failed due to the passage of time and possibly inability to get sufficient purchase.

As we were due to go on holiday I asked my local garage if they would have a go. On picking up the car later they had spent about 1 hour just attempting to lubricate the offending parts (spindle and sleeve) with a further suggestion that I take it back after 500 miles for further 'treatment'. As this would have been immediately after the holiday I decided not to.

Certainly the lubrication worked if only temporarily and some more positive action was required. I then decided to attempt to drill through the sleeve from the top and to put a piece of pipe in through which could be dribbled '3 in 1' oil. You will realise that to get through in this manner required drilling first through the floor and then the frame.

A small pilot hole, drilled to find position was not quite right but from that it was possible to put the next hole in the right place. The pipe I intended to use was ¼ inch O.D. nylon and my ¼ inch drill was barely long enough. However, I eventually succeeded in drilling through the sleeve, placing the tube in position and dribbling some oil down it. Lo and behold! I have had no further trouble with this problem and only need to dribble oil occasionally. The top of the tube is sealed off with a small plug to prevent ingress of dirt.

With no lubrication access provided I hope this may be of help to other members experiencing the same problem

Alan Sterne

July 1985

CAM & ROCKER SHAFT

I read with great interest the article in last month's Overdrive on cam and rocker shaft removal, as I did this job myself a month previous on my 85,000 mile '95' and found badly worn rocker shafts. But I ignored the manual as far as drilling holes in the bulkhead to remove the rear shafts as both shafts can be removed from the front end with ease, with the aid of a Stan Johnstone Rapide removal tool. Which consists of a piece of tube slightly smaller than the shaft to be removed which will pass through the bearing surfaces and long enough to reach the shorter shaft once the longer front shaft has been removed. With an 'easy out' driven in or held in with an Allen screw in one end and a hole in the other for a (T) bar.

This job I did without too much difficulty on my own even though replacing rockers, followers, spacers and springs with one hand and pushing shaft back with the other, tested my back and my temper. But I must say that I think the manual leaves a lot to be desired on quite a few points during my fifteen years as a Rover owner.

R. J. Cundy   *July 1985*

GRAB-HANDLE RESTORATION

When I acquired my P4 the 'grab-handles' in the rear were very frayed and the metal tongue inside was showing through the material. Incidentally, these items, sometimes referred to as 'anklestraps' are in fact described as 'Pillar-Pulls' in the Parts Catalogue.

After removing them from the car, spring the chrome end to one side and you will find two more screws. They are usually tight, but once removed the strap can then be unfolded. If the tongue has split the material, the former can be stuck back with Evo-Stik to prevent the problem recurring.

Woolworths' Iron-on Tape can then be applied to the inside, after trimming any frayed edges with scissors. It is cheap, the right width and a good colour-match.

If necessary, clean the outside with Decosol, or spray upholstery-cleaner (which keeps the material drier). Chrome-cleaner will probably do wonders for the end-assembly, then all that remains is to reassemble and screw them back in the car.

Alan Gilham   *September 1985*

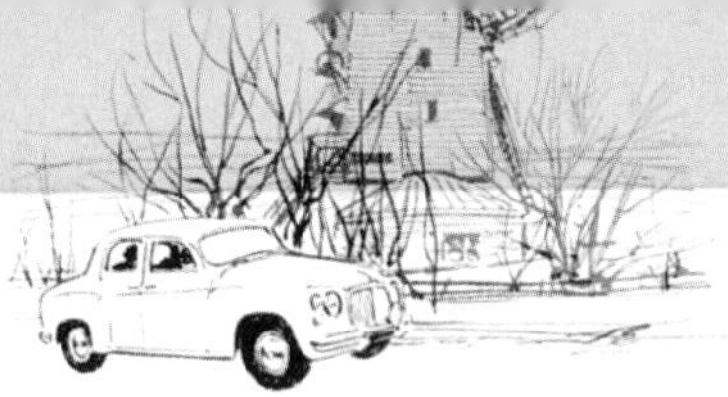

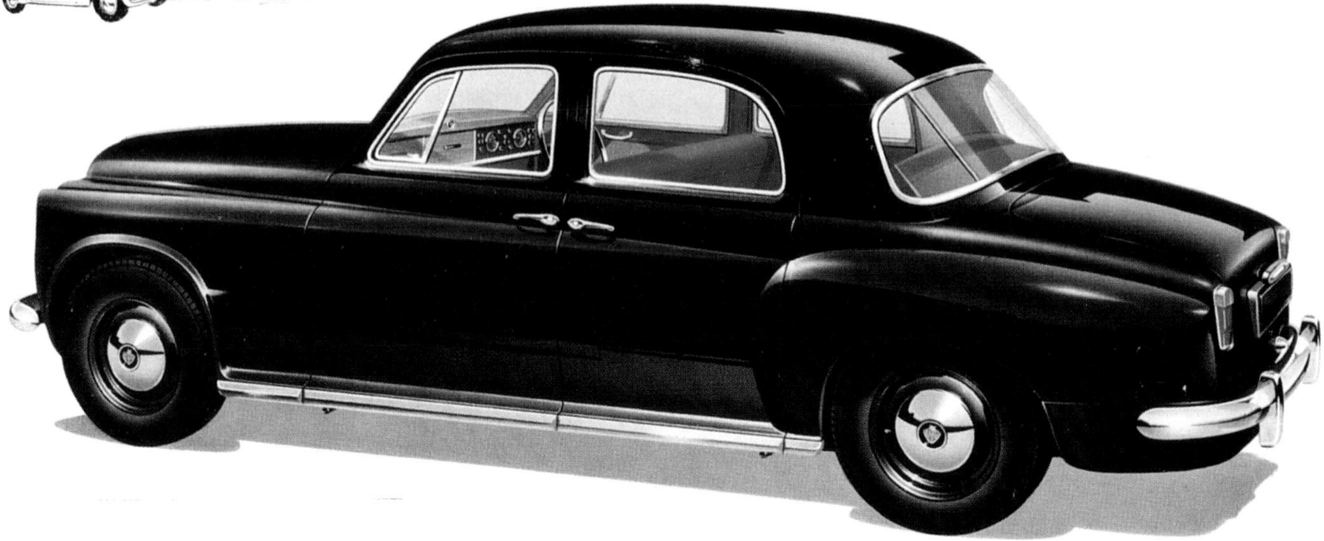

THE ROVER 75

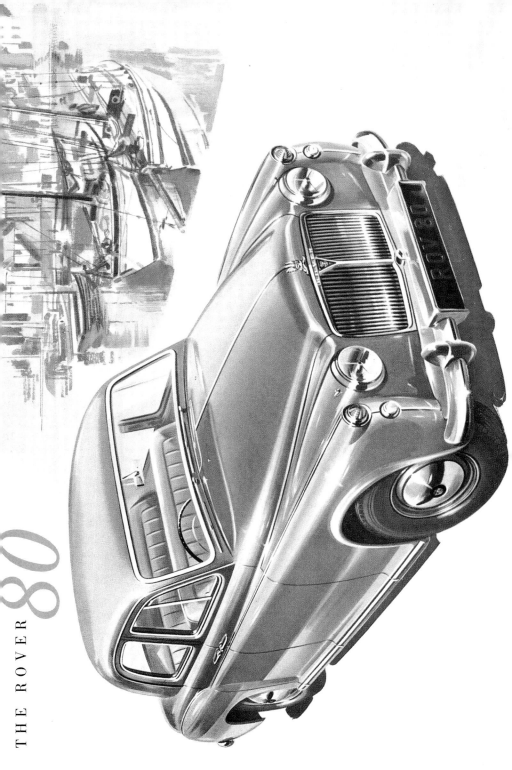

THE ROVER *80*

TIPS

I can offer the following method of replacing the spire clip slotted plates which have a maddening tendency to tear away from the hardboard base of the trim panels because the clips have rusted into the door itself.

The only things required are a 4 BA taper tap, obtainable from any good ironmonger and some 4 BA counter-sunk headed screws.

It will be found that the slotted plates have built-in hollow rivets, these will accept the 4 BA tap with no trouble, the only other thing is a small piece of tin plate – a bit of treacle-tin lid will serve very well. Drill it to correspond with the holes in the slotted plate, ease the rexine, or leather back on the edge of the door over the affected part, slip the tin plate in under the covering, insert screws, trim off any excess thread, re-glue the trim and you have a repair stronger than new.

F. L. Pearson

September 1985

SERVICE YOUR WATERWORKS!

Now's the time to give a bit of thought to your P4's cooling system before the winter sets in (have we had summer yet I hear you ask?!!). In view of the excessive rainfall we've had in the last couple of months, I don't think your Local Water Authority would object to you using a few gallons in giving the waterworks a good flushing.

In actual fact, the Rover's system should ideally be flushed twice yearly, but if it is done religiously once a year without missing a year occasionally, this should suffice. I am making a point in saying this because having chatted to various members in the past they look at me aghast when I mention that I've just done my yearly flush. Some in fact, believe that anti-freeze lasts forever. The system must have at least 5 pints of anti-freeze in it at all times and should be replaced with new every year. Having a cast iron block and an aluminium cylinder head, this creates a 'dissimilar' situation which encourages corrosion and the inhibitors in the anti-freeze help to control this. Plain water, especially in an area with 'hard water' will rapidly corrode the waterways particularly the aluminium head, thermostat housing and water pump.

Thermostats do not go on for ever either and should be renewed every two years. Incidentally, it is imperative to fit an alcohol filled bellows type which always fails safe (open) as opposed to the waxstat type which fails closed. This of course can lead to excessive heat developing in the head and be a possible cause of warping and blown head gasket. It is never wise to run without a thermostat, as not only will you have a tepid heater in the winter, but the engine will not run very efficiently without it. Plus, an overcooled engine can tend to increase the petrol consumption slightly too.

Several days prior to flushing the system it pays to add a proprietary de-scaling compound to the cooling water and immediately after a run, open the drain taps on the radiator and block and allow to drain. If the flow seems slow, probe the taps with a length of wire. Once drained, release the bottom hose at the water pump connection pipe and place a garden hose in to the top of the radiator. Turn on the water from the tap and adjust the rate of flow to allow as much water as possible through the radiator and out through the bottom hose without making too much mess of your engine compartment.

Allow this to run for about fifteen minutes and then reverse flush the radiator by placing the hose in to the bottom hose and allow the water to run up the rad and out through the filler at the header tank. Again allow the water to run for about fifteen minutes. That should take care of the radiator, now you can concentrate on the engine.

Start by removing the top hose and then the thermostat and its housing. Ideally, it is better not to force any sludge through the heater box, so the heater should be cleaned separately from the engine block. The heater can be bi-passed by removing the two hoses from the heater and linked together with a short length of ½ inch copper pipe. This may seem a bit of a chore but it will leave the system as clean as possible and once done, it will be quicker to carry out on subsequent flushes. Wedge the garden hose in to the empty thermostat aperture and adjust water flow to allow the fastest circulation without spilling back out of the top. If possible, run the water for about half and hour, with a drain nearby, or course, and the bottom hose still disconnected.

This done, the heater can then be flushed by attaching the hose to the pipe at the top of the heater box and to save making a mess of your engine, attach a short length of hose to the bottom pipe and direct down on to the road. Run water for about ten minutes and then reverse the pipes and force the water up through heater until clean water is coming through the box.

Replace and tighten hoses having checked that they are in good condition. Leave the heater hose disconnected from the top of the heater. Check that the valve is open on the heater (if it is still operative!). Replace thermostat using a new gasket and with both the drain taps closed, slowly fill the system with water, adding the anti-freeze as you go. Fill until water starts to escape through the disconnected hose at the top of the heater. Connect and tighten hose and run the engine until hot water can be felt passing through the top hose, showing that the thermostat has opened. Check for leaks and with the engine still running undo the top hose on the heater box until a steady flow of water is running from it, with no air bubbles, and then replace and tighten the hose.

Take the car for a test run keeping a watchful eye on the temperature gauge. Check under the bonnet on your return just to see that you have no leaks. You will have to wait until the first winter's night before you are rewarded for your work with nice warm feet.

Stan Johnstone   *September 1985*

RENOVATION OF INTERIOR DOOR TRIM

First remove the inside moulding (2 s.t. screws in front top and rear channels or through front window surround in front doors) and carefully ease out the moulding. I would suggest covering the gap in the top of the door with a cloth to prevent the screws disappearing inside.

Remove the door and window regulator handles by prising back the cap over the coil spring and pushing out the retaining pins with a suitable punch, followed by the door pull. Remove the small s.t. screws under the moulding which hold the top of the door casing.

The casing is now retained by spire clips and two s.t. screws (front doors only) which retain the spring wire which keeps the top of the door pocket taut. Ease out the spire clips with a long broad bladed screwdriver placed close to each clip. If you are just removing the door casing to gain access to the interior of the door ease the casing away from the door whilst unscrewing the s.t. screws at the top of the pocket. This leaves the screws in the casing and does not release the spring wire.

Replacement is the reversal of the above. When replacing the moulding fix masking tape to the moulding adjoining the metal tags and mark the alignment of the hole on the tape. This enables the screws to be more easily located in their holes.

The cloth trim at the bottom of my doors was badly discoloured and rotten. Material of the correct colour was not available so it was necessary to purchase the lightest available shade of beige and proceed to a friendly dyeworks to obtain the required shade of green.

Remove the old trim from the hardboard and then carefully dismantle into individual items making careful note of how it was originally assembled, otherwise you will be in trouble. Sew in the new material as necessary which is easier said than done, taking care not to over-stretch – I used a domestic treadle machine.

Fix trim to the hardboard and re-assemble taking care to ensure that the eyes at each end of the spring will have the s.t. screws passed through them.

You should now have a smart door casing.

Derek Humphreys   *January 1986*

THOUGHTS ON LUBRICATION

The P4 being as robust and well engineered as can be will stand up to all kinds of abuse but its achilles heel, like all machines, is its inability to keep going without regular lubrication at all points. I hope the following views will be of use and of interest.

The Engine:

As I mentioned before, the engine oil should be changed every 3,000 miles. This is most important because beyond this point the oil deteriorates rapidly. You only have to rub the old oil between your fingers to notice how thin and 'dry' it becomes after a few thousand miles. The filter has also to be changed. I have heard people say they change the oil at 3,000 miles and the filter at 6,000 miles. i.e. change filter every other oil change. I personally don't think this is good practice as a clogged filter just gets by-passed and becomes useless allowing all the damaging silt to circulate round the engine. Good quality oil should be used as opposed to the cheaper varieties to be found in the supermarkets.

I like to think that the nearest modern equivalent to the oil originally specified, i.e. Castrol XL, is Castrol GTX. However any good multigrade oil is usable in the 20/50 range but I think the new 10/40 oils are a shade too 'thin' for P4's.

The Gearbox:

The gearbox oil should be changed every couple of years or at about 20,000 miles. The handbooks can be a bit misleading because at one time a 90 E.P. grade was recommended and then in later editions a 20 S.A.E. oil is stated. This came about because of a rather sluggish overdrive operation in very cold conditions using 90 E.P. So a 20 grade oil was them said to be better for all weather conditions. In actual fact both oils do the job but, of course, E.P. oils were really intended for the meshing of gears, so I think it is probably better than 20 S.A.E. This is particularly true if the seals on the gearbox are a little bit suspect.

The Rear Axle:

Some people seem to think the oil in the differential lasts forever. Whilst it does have a long life it does break down eventually. Therefore it should be changed every 20,000 miles or so. After a high mileage the oil becomes full of tiny particles of metal and if allowed to churn around between the gears, premature wear will ensue and lead to the dreaded 'whine from the back'.

Steering Box and Idler:

The steering box should be checked once a year and topped up with 140 (if you can still find it) or 90 E.P. If the seal is defective either replace it if possible or check and top up at regular intervals. The idler shaft needs topping with the same grade of oil just to the top of the bore of the shaft, no more or you will force the oil through the seal, when you replace the nut.

Swivel Pins:

I have of course, gone into detail before on swivel pins, but just to reiterate on what I said before, I think the ideal lubricant is a mixture of 20/50 and molyslip. This is slightly thinner than the 140 stipulated but it does encourage the oil to 'creep' more and therefore reach the parts other oils cannot reach! 90 E.P. oil will do the job just as good. These should be checked at least twice a year.

Front Wheel Hubs:

Again it must be stressed that lubricants do not last forever and ideally the front hubs should be removed every 20,000 miles and washed thoroughly in paraffin and replenished with new high-melting point grease. Incidentally,

LM on a tin of Castrol grease means high melting point. Never did quite understand that! Do not over-tighten the hub bearings as this will only result in excessive heat and cook the grease. Always back off one hole when the nut has just bitten onto the bearing.

The Propshaft:

Don't forget the poor old propshaft. An occasional grease should be applied to the sliding section of the shaft and on earlier models to the universal joints as well.

All these lubricating jobs can be a chore I know, but they do keep the wheels turning and your Rover will go on indefinitely with a regular servicing routine. Incidentally 'Hermetite' are now producing a straight 20 oil in handy bottles to top up the damper or dampers on your S.U. carburettors. This is much better than 20/50 which is really too heavy or 3 in 1 which is too thin.

I keep a small notebook in my car and keep a check on the various lubricating jobs otherwise it is surprising how the miles build up and you can never remember when you last checked your various P4 duties.

Stan Johnstone   *January 1986*

BAKELITE—THE CURE FOR HOT S.U.'s

Reference to your hot starting problems mentioned in your editorial in Overdrive 45.

I experienced the same problem on my 1951 Cyclops and found the reason is vapour locks building up in the carburettors (not in the Cyclop's engine-bay-mounted fuel pump as might have been expected). Obviously the carbs got too hot after several minutes of rest (without the cooling air stream of the radiator fan) and the symptoms were exactly as you describe them.

The cure was to isolate the carburettors from the cylinder head: bakelite plates were cut to the same shape as the flange gaskets and were fitted together with two gaskets between carb. body and cylinder head. On my 75 the bolts are just long enough to accept the additional thickness of the bakelite (about 4mm thick), Thin isolating washers were fitted under the nuts to prevent heat flowing to the carbs via the bolts and nuts.

This treatment completely cured the troubles several years ago. When you look into the engine bays of modern cars, in most cases you will find isolating pieces between carburettor and head, so the problem seems to be quite common.

Michael Mayr-Harting, Austria

January 1986

HOW'S YOUR AUNTIE?

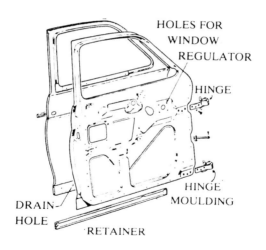

1. The drainage of water from within the doors is intended to be by way of several drainage holes behind the stainless steel mouldings which run along the bottom of each door. These mouldings are held to the doors by 4 or 5 retainers, the nuts on which are accessible along the inner side of the doors when in the open position.

At Auntie's age blockages can occur so that water may remain inside the doors for quite a long time. A clear-out is worthy of recommendation.

To aid removal of the mouldings it is worthwhile to carefully wirebrush the exposed ¼" dia. threads and nuts, and soak with penetrating oil before attempting to undo the retainer fastenings. It is probable that 1 in 4 of the retainer threads will shear off, even when care is taken to progress carefully. It is not essential that every retainer is replaced on completion of the work but the margin for losses is not so great that some spare retainers should not be considered.

When the moulding is removed from a door the drainage holes in the door can be cleaned out. The moulding can also be cleaned out after each seized retainer is given a light tap and slid to the moulding end where the slotted moulding form enlarges to allow removal. The retainers can be scraped of scale, and the threads wirebrushed and waxoyl applied generously.

With all surfaces cleaned the moulding(s) can be replaced and the reward found to be that rainwater will run out at the ends of the moulding as originally intended.

2. The weight of the wind-up window glass in a door is considerable. It is *not* supported directly beneath the glass but by the 4 screw attachment to the door's inner panel, but so to speak, at arm's length. In the case of aluminium R.H. front (driver's) doors – most models, the holes in the inner panel can become considerably elongated by the pressure exerted by the setscrews which have not remained tightly fastened.

WINDOW REGULATOR (WINDER)

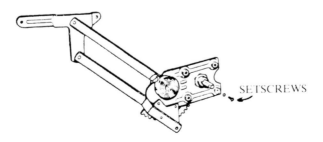

SETSCREWS

The window, receiving less support, will have started to lean against the rearmost support channel. If the window whilst not fully wound-up is lifted

Drilling Pedal Spindle

The use of a lathe is required for this exercise. Any garage or engineering firm with turning facilities can easily carry out this task.

PEDAL SPINDLE

Hole 'A' — Centre drill in lathe then drill ⅛" diameter to a depth equal to ¾" beyond housing bearing position. (Fig. 3).
Hole 'B' — Drill ⅛" diameter in brake pedal fixing bolt groove intersecting with Hole 'A'.
Hole 'C' — Drill ⅛" diameter ½" beyond bearing position (Fig. 3) intersecting with Hole 'A'.
Carefully remove any burrs with fine file and polish spindle with fine emery cloth.
Check fit in housing.

FITTING OIL NIPPLE

Fitting Oil Nipple (Refer to Fig. 4)

Take brake pedal lever and using centre punch pop mark the middle of space between lever for pedal rod and master cylinder operating lever in alignment with centre of hole for lever fixing bolt. Drill ¹³⁄₆₄" diameter and thread hole ¼" BSF using tap and tap wrench. Carefully deburr hole in bore of pedal bush. Fit standard ¼ BSF straight grease nipple and check fit on spindle. Ensure blanking plug is secure by giving smart tap in centre with light hammer.

Reassembly

Clean all components.
If oil seals in housing are badly worn now is the time to replace (9 and 10 Fig. 1).

Reassembly — reverse of stripping procedure.
With a grease gun containing EP90 or similar oil, inject oil via nipple into housing, by careful feel keep injecting oil until resistance is felt – when air is expelled and housing full of oil.

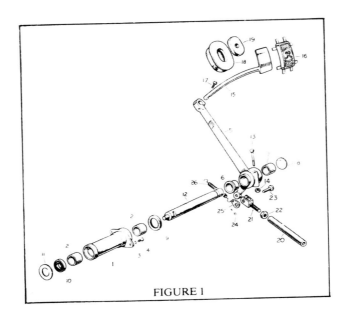

FIGURE 1

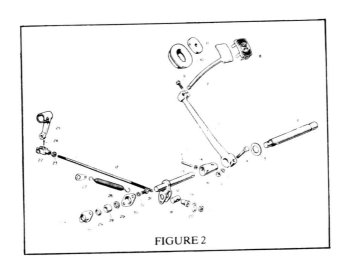

FIGURE 2

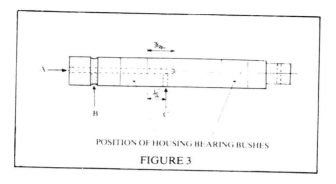

POSITION OF HOUSING BEARING BUSHES

FIGURE 3

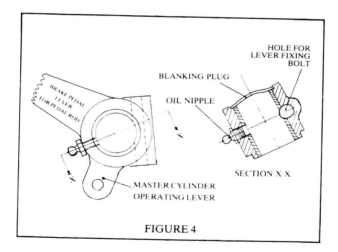

FIGURE 4

Conclusion

You will now have smooth pedal operation transmitting the correct feel to your boot as when new. By simple, quick attention at six monthly intervals to make up any loss of oil precise pedal operation will be maintained.

Andy Doe

November 1986

GET OUT AND GET UNDER

I, too, have been painting the underside of my P4 and heartily endorse the "little bit at a time and stick to it" advice you gave in your November editorial.

At first I found the sight of my '100' so daunting from below, as it stretched away into the distance, that I very nearly didn't start at all. But little by little, an hour or so at a time, transistor radio at my side, I have wirebrushed and scraped, Jenolited and Smoothrited, until – I have to admit – things are looking really quite presentable down there. I now have a pleasing speckled appearance and the family are expert at holding conversations with my feet. But to my surprise I've enjoyed it, at least until the chill striking up from the concrete garage floor, even through a couple of layers of old carpet, becomes too much. Then I retire indoors to commune with the teapot and restore my circulation. Until the next small step.

One of the most useful aids to this multi-stage marathon has been a household radiator paintbrush – the type with a long wire handle. This you can bend in any number of permutations to get at the host of "important little places" that lie in wait to challenge the P4 owner, especially round the battery box and rear outriggers. Combined with a couple of artists' brushes, I've found I can easily reach the parts other brushes, etc.

I suspect you'll be reporting the completion of your "paint job" long before I'm half way finished, but I'm determined to make it . . . . . "a little bit at a time".

Dennis Jones   *January 1989*

FUEL PUMPS

I have recently had to have new contacts fitted to the main SU petrol pump in my Rover '100'.

In order to keep the car on the road I wished to remove the main pump for servicing, but to retain the reserve pump in use, which meant blanking off the pipes to the main pump.

I therefore made the plugs (2) which are detailed on the enclosed sketch. As it turned out to be a job requiring certain vital dimensions, I thought it might be of interest to '100' owners to know the details.

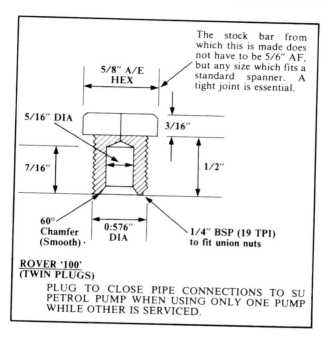

The stock bar from which this is made does not have to be 5/6" AF, but any size which fits a standard spanner. A tight joint is essential.

5/8" A/E HEX

5/16" DIA

3/16"

7/16"

1/2"

60° Chamfer (Smooth) ·

0:576" DIA

1/4" BSP (19 TPI) to fit union nuts

ROVER '100' (TWIN PLUGS)

PLUG TO CLOSE PIPE CONNECTIONS TO SU PETROL PUMP WHEN USING ONLY ONE PUMP WHILE OTHER IS SERVICED.

K. Stocker

March 1989

ROVER OVERDRIVE ELECTRICAL CIRCUIT

The Rover '80' and '100' overdrive system incorporates some rather unusual and elegant electrical circuitry which merits explanation. The unusual feature is the way in which the overdrive relay coil is de-energised when the overdrive is disengaged. Instead of the relay coil being de-energised by switching off its current, which is the normal method, the relay coil is de-energised initially by applying battery voltage (-12v) to each end of its coil.

The complete electrical operating sequence of the overdrive is as follows:

Overdrive disengaged

The overdrive switch on the steering column is OFF; so there is no current path from the overdrive fuse, through the overdrive relay coil or solenoid coil, to the bottom earth line; hence, both the relay and solenoid remain de-energised. The ball valve in the overdrive hydraulic system, which is operated by the overdrive solenoid, remains seated. Refer to page C18 of the overdrive manual for an explanation of the overdrive hydraulic system.

Select Overdrive Engaged

Before the overdrive can be engaged, the gearbox switch must be closed by having top gear selected; and both throttle switches must be closed.

The throttle switch with the vertical plunger is set so that it is *closed* when the throttle is between 0 and one half open. The throttle switch with the horizontal plunger is set so that it is *open* when the throttle is between 0 and one eighth open. Therefore, for both switches to be closed, the throttle must be between one eighth and one half open.

Having engaged top gear and set the throttle so that both switches are closed, overdrive is engaged by moving the steering column switch down to ON. This makes the circuit from the overdrive fuse, through the relay coil and relay resistance, to the horizontal earth line at the bottom, thereby energising the relay.

When the relay is energised, the RL contact closes so that current flows through the overdrive solenoid coil, thereby energising the solenoid.

When the solenoid is energised, it lifts the ball valve off its seat to direct high pressure oil to the overdrive operating pistons.

Kickdown

When the kick-down switch beneath the accelerator is operated by pressing the accelerator hard down, the KICK TO CLOSE switch closes. This applies battery voltage to both ends of the overdrive relay coil, thereby neutralising (de-energising) the coil and causing the RL contact to open. This breaks the feed to the solenoid coil and de-energises the solenoid. The ball valve reseats to shut off the oil supply to the overdrive operating pistons, and allows the oil from the pistons to pass to exhaust; the overdrive then moves into disengagement.

On releasing the kick-down switch, the system reverts to its previous state.

Select Overdrive Disengaged

When the steering column switch is moved to off, battery voltage is applied to the lower end of the relay coil, via the horizontal plunger throttle switch (providing the throttle is more than one eighth open) and the OFF terminal on the selector switch. As battery voltage is also being applied to the top of the relay coil, the coil is neutralised and therefore de-energised, which in turn de-energises the solenoid by the opening of the RL contact.

Once the RL contact opens, the circuit between the overdrive fuse and the bottom earth line is broken. The de-energising of the solenoid reseats the ball valve, so that the hydraulic oil is released as previously described and the overdrive moves into disengagement.

Mike Austin

March 1989

COOLING DOWN YOUR P4

I have been asked many times for advice on the problem of overheating on the P4. I have also read articles in the Overdrive of members who have gone to great lengths to solve the problem, one member ended up fitting an expansion tank return system. Others run around without the thermostat.

Let's get one thing straight, apart from the 1950 to 1953 cars, no P4 should overheat, if it does then something is wrong, let's face it, it is, compared with modern day cars, a low pressure water system, it has approx. two gallons of water, and two gallons of oil. I mention oil, because apart from its lubricating properties it is also used as a coolant.

Let's look at what could be causing the overheating.

Thermostat – always worth replacing.

Blocked or partially blocked radiator.

Ignition timing and valve timing.

Carburettor settings.

Head gasket leaking.

Brakes binding making the engine labour.

Slipping fan belt.

Water pump.

Assuming that the average P4 owner being a type of person that keeps his car in good service order, has had all the above checked, is still scratching his head, the following could well help in solving the problem.

First drain the system completely, i.e. both drain taps, flush through fresh water via a hose from a water supply, reverse flow the flushing by putting the end of the hose pipe over the block tap and then the radiator tap, yes, I'm sorry this will probably make a mess of your polished engine compartment, but never mind, after the flushing and there is no more sediment or brown coloured water coming out let the system completely drain down. Close the two taps, make up your mixture of good quality anti-freeze of at least 33⅓% but these days it is recommended a mixture of 50% is correct, remember, anti-freeze has properties built into it to protect engines from corrosion and overheating, on modern vehicles anti-freeze is left in all year round and is mixed at 50%, there is no reason for not giving your P4 the same protection, especially with our aluminium heads etc. It must of course be checked from time to time for strength. Fill via the radiator cap slowly allowing the mixture to circulate and settle, keep topping up, have the heater controls on the dash set to hot, when you think the system is full, put your hand down and compress the bottom hose, do this several times, working it like a pump, you should see air bubbles and movement in the top of the radiator, when the air bubbles have stopped, check and top up the radiator again, never fill to the neck of the filler, always allow at least ½" to ¾" below the neck, fit the radiator cap and start the engine, allow to reach normal temperature, check for leaks and allow to idle, switch off after 15 minutes, allow the system to cool down, check and top up if required.

The last point, and I am not having a dig at the Rally and show members who only take their P4's out in the summer, but I can't help noticing the numbers of cars with the heat control left in the off position, air locks do occur in engines from time to time, and leaving the control in the off position does no good, firstly by having the control in the hot position allows the cooling water to circulate through the heater matrix and helps to keep it clean, and secondly, by allowing the coolant to properly circulate throughout the engine. I have often cured a member's problem of overheating by opening the control to the hot position and taking the car for a run, take a container of coolant with you, because you may find your temperature gauge doing funny things, if it does, stop, allow the engine to cool down, and then top up the radiator as described. You don't of course have to run around all summer with the heater on, you can of course return it to the off position, or have it in the hot position with the main control knob in the fresh air position, this allows water to pass through the matrix, but not into the car.

If as I do, you tow a caravan, you will find after a long drive in hot conditions, or climbing long hills, i.e. Dorset, Cornwall etc., the temperature gauge will increase to the middle of the white position, but should not go into the red.

Ian Jones   *September 1989*

NOTES ON FITTING A RADIO CASSETTE TO A P4 '110'

I can think of no very good reason why a car like the P4 should not be updated with the latest gadgets in modern technology as long as it is done with discretion and taste. I have fitted to my own P4, radials, quartz lamps and electronic ignition and it is none the worse for it and I certainly feel just that little bit safer as a result. I thought a good quality radio would be a worthwhile addition and so this is a blow-by-blow account of what is entailed.

All the radios you can buy now are negative earth so you will have to reverse the polarity of the car before you switch on the set. Take out the battery and put on one side for the moment. Drop the battery leads below the car and remove the lugs. These must now be fitted to the opposite cables. Gettit? My P4 had integral lugs and there was no way of saving them so they had to be sacrificed (you can melt them off with a heavy-duty soldering iron). I had to fit another neg. lead because the original one was too short (you have to turn the battery round 180° which means the neg. lead will be too short to reach the neg. post on the battery. Are you still with me? NOW and this is MOST IMPORTANT – TAPE UP THE ARMOURED CONDUIT ON THE LEAD WHICH WHEN FINISHED WILL BE GOING TO THE POS. LUG. THIS WILL PREVENT THE CONDUIT CREEPING ALONG THE CABLE AND CREATING A SHORT-CIRCUIT. So much for the battery.

Now for the clock.

My clock has two wires going to it which means that the '110' owner does not need to alter the wiring. Owners of lesser vehicles which have only one wire feeding the clock (and here I refer only to power supply NOT the wire feeding the bulb) will have to remove the clock, insulate it completely and reconnect it. TAKE EXPERT LOCAL ADVICE ON THIS MATTER!

Now the dynamo.

Re-polarise the dynamo by letting the engine idle and close the cut-out points. If you then open the throttle slightly you should see a discharge on the ammeter. Let the instrument panel down and change over the connections on the ammeter. And that's the dynamo done!

Now for the aerial.

USE THE PROPER ONE – nothing looks worse than the wrong aerial on a car like the Rover. (At first I fitted a stick-on aerial to the inside of the windscreen – it looked neat and unobtrusive but it didn't work!) Eventually I fitted one I had had on a P6 and it looks a treat! Take off the visors, the mirror, the narrow bit of head-lining and the windscreen moulding. You will then see a hole of about 4 inches in diameter. Find the centre of this and drill a hole through the roof to match your aerial mounting. Fit the aerial remembering to put some sealing compound between it and the roof and lead the wire down the side of the screen to the back of the dash. DON'T FORGET TO SCRAPE THE PAINT OFF WHERE YOU MAKE YOUR EARTH CONNECTIONS. I had to drill another hole at the top corner of the screen to get the wire tucked away neatly. This done, head-lining, visors, moulding and mirror can be put back.

Now for the speakers.
  Because all sets nowadays are stereophonic you have two speakers which in my case were square because I thought they would be easier to fit. I put these under the front seats out of the way, each one in a hardwood box which, according to the experts in 'in-car entertainment' has the effect of throwing the sound forward. I suspended them from the frame of the seat by 'L' shaped pieces of mild steel. Drill a hole in the bottom of each box and take the leads under the carpet up to the set.

Now for the receiver.
  Take off the middle cupboard door (which is NOT solid mahogany as the Road Test Report would have you believe) and substitute a veneered piece of ply (or even solid mahogany!). The cardboard pocket and second bit of card will have to come out (you need all the depth you can get) and be discarded. Make two pieces of angle-iron and pop-rivet them vertically to the dashboard frame now exposed. The radio fascia board will be screwed to this using self-tapping screws which, unhappily, are not brass finished. Cut a hole in this board and feed the set through a line-fuse from the vacant terminal on the ignition switch. The set should be earthed to the chassis of the car.
  Remember, you get what you pay for, as in everything. I bought Radiomobile in the fond, perhaps vain hope that it was not Japanese owned.
  Suppressing the dynamo, coil, etc. will have to be done on an empirical basis.

R Jessop   *November 1989*

P4 DOOR HINGES

As members are aware door hinges eventually wear and the pins can even fracture resulting in sagging and rattling doors. Repair of the hinges, when removed, is not difficult provided one has and can use the necessary equipment – it is their removal when bolts have rusted and the bottom of the front wing is in a fragile state which causes problems. However it is a job worth doing so proceed as follows.

Remove the interior door handles by pressing out the retaining pins whilst holding back the spring loaded escutcheons. Remove door mouldings – the front mouldings have four S.T. screws in the glass run channel and two in the front face of the door and the rear doors have all six screws in the glass run channel. The door casing is then removed, this being retained at the top by S.T. screws under the moulding, 2 S.T. screws at the top of the door pockets on the front doors and numerous spire clips. Do not remove the screws at the top of the pocket from the casing otherwise you will lose the ends of the expanding curtain wires which control the opening of the door pocket. When prising out spire clips, make sure the screwdriver or tyre lever actually contacts the clip before exerting pressure as this reduces the possibility of the clip retainer pulling out of the hardboard. Remove the pin from the check strap and then the bolts securing the hinges to the door noting the position of any shims.

Front Hinges

Remove the A post rubber retainer – S.T. screws, and the set bolts securing the rear of the wing to the A post and the bottom of the wing below the wheelarch moulding thus enabling the bottom of the wing to be pulled outwards taking care at the same time to release the rubber seal between wing and splash panel which will be stuck to the wing with underseal. Remove the scuttle trim panel from inside the car again retained by spire clips. The Workshop Manual says pull back the end of the sill mat to gain access to the retaining screw underneath but I find it preferable to remove the mat. It is now possible to gain access to the hinge fixings – upper hinge, two screws in the face of the A post and a nut accessible behind the scuttle panel – lower hinge, one screw in the face of the A post, one bolt through the sill with the nut usually well rusted and a nut accessible behind the wing.

Rear Hinges

Remove sill mat and stainless steel wheelarch moulding which is secured by a nut inside the wheelarch and a S.T. screw through the leading edge. The upper hinges are secured by two screws in the door post and two screws accessible through the hinge aperture. The lower hinges are secured by one screw in the face of the door post, a bolt through the sill and a nut behind the wheelarch moulding.

Repairing the hinges involves grinding off the welds securing the locating washers on each end of the pin, driving out the old pin, drilling and reaming to fit a suitable oversize pin and rewelding the locating washers to the new pin. Quite often the section of the hinge which bolts to the sill is rusted and requires repair by welding. Also make sure that the oil groove is clear to the pin.

Replacement is the reversal of the above but includes the additional work of correctly aligning doors and ensuring that the rubber seals inside the front wings are correctly positioned and sealed with underseal to prevent ingress of water.

You could well find on dismantling that further repairs are required to the sills in the vicinity of the front hinge boxes and also the wings behind the wheelarch mouldings.

I would be happy to repair hinges for members at very reasonable rates if they were forwarded to me.

Derek Humphreys   *January 1990*

WINDOW FRAMES AND CHANNELLING

It's worth doing both jobs at once as to do just one means removal of the other and both are tricky to remove and replace. All the screws in the channelling are difficult to get out, particularly those at the side rather than at the top as these have more moisture trickling past them over the years. A really sharp, square screwdriver is needed and perhaps a pre-soaking in WD40. Even then you will probably have to mutilate one or two screws but you may be lucky. Cherish the screws that you manage to remove as they are scarce. When you have all screws removed the wooden window frame and then the channel should come out. In my case the wood joints were all loose and with the moulding on the bench it was an easy task to prise the components apart keeping all the plywood fillets that join the corners. It's worth marking them or keeping them in the same position to aid re-assembly.

Clean all the old glue from the joint faces, the fillets and their grooves. Then re-assemble all the joints with woodglue and either clamp or bind the structure together until the glue is cured.

Obviously some care must be employed here to ensure that the structure is not twisted or otherwise misaligned. Once it is a complete and solid frame it is much easier to clean off the old varnish using a craft knife blade as a scraper and to smooth off with progressively finer sandpaper or wet and dry used dry. When you are satisfied with the surface clean off all dust with methylated spirits and allow to dry. I then used polyurethane varnish in about four coats, rubbed down between coats and finished off with a light going over of T-Cut or even Solvol to smooth the surface. Lastly put a bit of wax polish on the wood to protect further. It is important to varnish the inside edge that is visible from outside of the car when fitted, that is, the bit closest to the glass at the bottom. I of course only noticed this once the first window had been re-assembled. Originally the mouldings had a similar material to headlining wrapped around the inner section – presumably to alleviate rattling or draughts. This went under the metal tabs that attach the moulding to the door. I replaced this with black felt glued in place. The tabs are of course cleaned and painted and replaced. So now you should have the mouldings complete.

Now to the door and channelling. You should already have the channel out and this will give you access to clean up any corrosion present on the aluminium (or steel) – removing draught strips, cleaning and painting as you go. The channelling that is currently available from specialist automotive suppliers has no chrome strips; it is black all over but is very easy to handle, cut and bend, and produces a lovely smooth operation that is entirely draught free. Its construction is an improvement on the old type as the illustrations show. It would be necessary to drill through the back of the old type in order to fit the screws. With the new ladder type it is only necessary to choose a slot that is closest to the existing holes in the door and push the screw through. The whole 'ladder' is covered in a malleable rubber material rather similar to Dum-Dum that stretches easily for sharp bends. It is necessary either to use the old channel as a pattern or measure accurately so that the ends of the channelling fit snugly into the vertical glass runners. Cutting is easy, simply flatten the channel at the relevant point as in Fig. 2 and with snips or heavy scissors or pliers snip at points A and as the rest is either felt or rubber, scissors will easily cut through. It can then be bent back to shape without damage. Achieving the curves for the door aperture is a matter of trial and error and it is worth spending a bit of time to get it right. The flexible channel is held in place by two screws only but the moulding has six screws on the rear doors that attach it. Having affixed the channel it is worth, using a wax pencil, marking the outer surface of the wood to indicate the positions of the metal tabs. Offer up the moulding to the door and carefully push the tabs between the channelling and door. Using a narrow but sharp bradawl or other tool line up the holes in the tabs with those on the door and the channel utilising a suitably placed slot. It is inevitable that some will not line up but the forgiving construction of the channel will allow a screw to be inserted at an angle and still do the job without fouling the glass. The bradawl is important as an aid to line up the position for the screw. Use a nice sharp screwdriver of the correct size and the job will be easier. I bought about 180 inches of the channel which is more than you need but will allow for a mistake in measuring, and this cost less than twenty pounds.

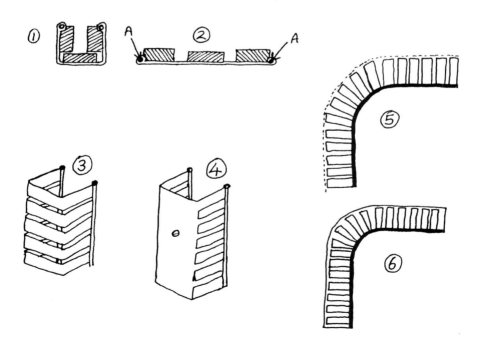

Key to Illustrations

1) Cross section of the flexible window channel
2) Flattened channel ready for cutting at points A
3) Skeletal view of new type channel – screws are inserted through suitable slot
4) Old type channel with solid back that would require drilling
5) New type and 6) old type channel at fairly acute bend, i.e. forward edge of rear door. The stretchy rubber on 5) covers the ladder even at the apex of the curve. Old type channel would need care to bend accurately

Have a go and say goodbye to rattly, draughty old windows for another thirty years!

Matt White

November 1990

P6 SU CONVERSION FOR THE '80'

Much interest was shown in Pat Moores P6 SU conversion for the '80' so he has put together the following notes to help you carry it out.

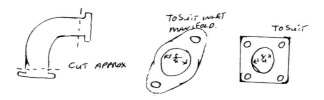

Firstly the manifold adaptor – I used a 2" plumbers elbow, which I cut down as small as possible in order to get the carburettor close to the manifold. The adaptor plates were made from $\frac{5}{16}$" thick mild steel plate, gaskets were used as templates to make these.

When complete, the adaptor plates were brazed to the elbow at the appropriate positions.

The air filter was adapted using an SU Carb pipe and a piece of 3" tube and original parts.

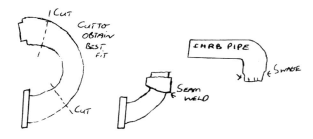

Throttle Linkage

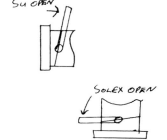

The flexible drive on the linkage must be replaced by a solid piece of bar because the SU throttle opens the opposite way to the Solex; causing the cable to unwind on the flexible drive.

The pedal linkage should be altered on the bulkhead to suit.

The linkage is all trial and error to obtain the best setting. An additional spring was also fitted to assist the throttle return.

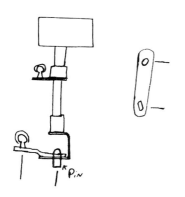

A bearing arm for the throttle linkage was made, using a piece of steel and a bronze bush.

The bearing arm was fitted to the car using one of the manifold studs.

Two levers were made keeping the hole centres equal.

Bearing arm slot for adjustment

The SU Carburettor pipe was cut to give the best fit, as close to 90° as possible and welded. The '80' piece of pipe was cut and swaged to fit into the SU Carburettor pipe. I used blind nuts to fix in place.

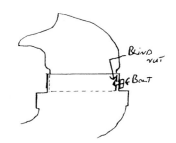

The flexible hose is too short to reach the carb so a piece of 3" tube was used to lengthen this.

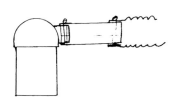

I cut the tube and closed down one end to fit inside the flexible hose and closed the tube down to fit outside the Air Filter. Once I had determined the sizes the tube was drilled and riveted. Then sealer was applied.

Leave out rivet for jubilee clip to clamp.

Pat Moores

November 1990

THE WAVERING SPEEDOMETER – THE TRUTH!

I was following the sorry tales and experiences of people with this problem and was actually dismayed having read an article from some expert advocating change of the speedo cable. The greasing or changing the cable will alleviate the wavering for a period of time but very seldom cure it. The reason is that the cable itself is not the cause of the problem, it is actually suffering from it! For the speedometer needle to register properly the two ends of the cable must run at the same speed (rpm) at any time while the car is rolling, any increase or decrease at the bottom (driving) end must be picked up at the top end, which in turn rotates the speedometer.

If and when a load/braking effect is applied to the top end, the cable will twist, and run slightly slower than the bottom end until it can twist no more, then it will spring forward, slow down again, spring forward etc. hence the wavering!

The cause of the extra load/braking effect is inside the speedometer unit but not the speedometer itself, the culprits are the two mileometers. Each one is driven from the main shaft by a worm-geared eccentric stepping lever. The drying out of lubricant in these two small components create the actual braking effect and the remedy is quite simple:

1. Remove speedometer taking care of the rubber ring behind the chrome bezel rim.

2. The chrome bezel is 'bayonet' fitted, looking from the back one can see which way to twist it for removal. When it is free the double glazed dial and a black surround will drop out with it.

3. Remove the two screws from the back of the unit and carefully withdraw the instrument.

From this point onward take care not to damage/bend the needle or the black face plate.

4. Remove the rubber seal (if fitted) from the back and the two gear wheels will be in view. At the outer end of each of these there is a curved, escutcheon fit spring leaf, holding the push lever and the shaft in place.

5. Press down the little 'mushroom' until the spring is flat and run in a small amount of 3-in-1 oil behind the gear wheel. Release and press again to work the oil in, add some more if necessary until movement is free, repeat on the other side.

5B. If there is no improvement the shaft will have to be removed for cleaning. CAUTION; Adjacent to the gears is the outer rim (aluminium) of the speedo movement, in no way must it be pressed upon!

With the aid of a pair of tweezers or small sharp nose pliers lift up the end of the spring leaf where the small hole is and gently push it towards the centre to disengage the escutcheon.

5C. Remove the lever gingerly so that the spring adjacent to the ratchet will stay anchored and just leave it hanging.

5D. Remove the small shaft with the gear wheel, clean the bore and the shaft with lighter fuel, methylated spirit (NOT WD40) oil it and reassemble.

6. Run small amount of oil behind worm drive and also the outer end of the square drive.

7. Replace rubber seal at the back, insert unit in the casing, fit two screws.

8. Fit black surround and double glazed dial with the small cut-out to the peg on casing.

9. Refit bezel, replace rubber ring behind bezel, refit Speedometer Unit.

To give you some idea of the duration, the first attempt should be less than an hour and a half, with some luck 30 minutes, most of which will be taken up by the removal and refitting of the speedometer to the dashboard.

Tom Tottis   *July 1991*

FITTING FLASHING INDICATORS TO PRE 1955 REAR LAMPS

In reply to Mark Kelly's request in last issue I herewith describe how to establish flashing indicators without making any external differences to appearance of the car. Please note that I only have flashing indicators at the rear. Because I could find no suitable lamp or bulb for the front that didn't spoil the 'originality' – that is white reflectors and the torpedo sidelamps – I perhaps should replace the white reflectors with late type (i.e. 1957 on) sidelamps with clear glass in the reflector position as Carl Haworth has done on his excellently restored 1953 '75' seen at Burghley House. Whichever you choose, the trafficators can still be used concurrently. The problem with only having rear flashers working is that the flasher unit needs to have two 21 watt bulbs drawing power from it to work properly. They will only flash dimly and very fast if one bulb is connected. So you need a redundant bulb for each side *and* a flasher unit for each side. Hiding these is not too difficult in the Rover boot compartment. The early type rear lamp has provision for a second bulb to encompass the lighting regulations for the American 'Dollar Area' export vehicles. On home vehicles the hole only is there and needs a suitable bulb holder fitting into it. I used holders from old broken rear lamps that I had in my collection of bits prising the bulb holders out, fitting them into the holes in the good lamps, pressing back the flanges and for good measure putting a dab of solder on the joint to ensure good contact. Whether the holders are two contact or one doesn't matter as you simply have to fit the correct bulb and run the wire to the appropriate contact – so stop-tail bulbs could be used as well as just single filaments. Incidentally – after making successful additions to the interiors of your lamps it is a good idea to paint the inside of the lamp body white and the bulb 'bracket' as well to improve brightness. They were white when new but are usually rather faded. So on to wiring. Using the single connection on the trafficator unit as your feed you can thread the wire over the door to appear at the rear of the rear door. Remove the lower quarter trim panel and a handy grommet will be revealed which is your route through to the boot compartment each side. To run wires forward should be a similar exercise – the wires appear inside and to the right of the fascia panel for the R/H side and behind the interior of the glove box for the L/H side hence through the bulkhead to frontlamps. In the boot compartment a good spot to hide a double bulb holder and two flasher units is underneath the filler pipe area. Make sure all connections are tight and wrap up with insulating tape for safety – and there you are – the only drawback is having these redundant bulbs lighting up the hidden recesses of your boot compartment, but it's better than having another car's sidelamps doing this for you.

*The advantage of having indicators in modern traffic is an obvious one as motorists these days can't be expected to see trafficators I suppose. It is good however to have them in operation just to show these modern cars how to turn a corner properly!

Matt White

July 1991

FLASHING INDICATORS ON EARLY P4's

The vexed question of how to discreetly include flashing indicators on early P4's has been posed many times, and our editor's modifications to his own 1954 '90' in this respect are well known. Without wishing to upset him, or anyone else who has done work in this area, I would like to submit the following solution to the problem, the result of which would be that one could, at the flick of a switch, change from trafficators to flashing indicators and vice versa. As relays and modifications to the wiring are involved, however, a certain fundamental knowledge of car electrics is needed; otherwise a local auto electrician should be able to do the job without much trouble. The modifications could be removed at a later date, if needed, leaving hardly a trace.

There are several problems to overcome:

1.   Switching arrangements.

2.   Incorporating indicator lamps.

3.   Incorporating a warning lamp.

Switching arrangements

The problem here is that three circuits need to be switched over together. Firstly, the feed to the trafficator switch needs to be diverted to go through a flasher unit, as on later models. Next, the current from the trafficator switch needs to be diverted to the indicator lamps instead of the trafficators (one switch for each side). One could just use three switches, of course, but a much neater arrangement would be a bank of three relays, mounted out of sight behind the dash panel, and operated by a single switch.

For those not familiar with relays, and I apologise for boring those who are, they are basically a sophisticated switch, capable of carrying quite a high current, whilst only needing a small current to operate them, a bit like a solenoid. The relays involved here, however, need to be of the "changeover" type (my terminology), as opposed to the straightforward "on-off" type. They are used in many applications in modern cars, so shouldn't be hard to track down.

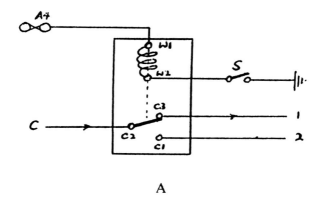

A

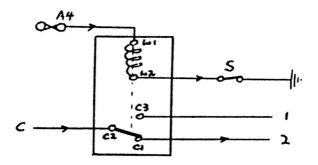

In illustration "A", with the relay off, the current "C" flows through it via terminals CS/C3 to circuit "1". When the relay is energised, however, (illustration "B"), by operating switch "S", the current is diverted via terminals C2/C1 to circuit "2". Thus it can be seen that not only can a simple "on/off" switch be used to perform the task, but that same switch can operate several relays simultaneously. The switch could, for example, be a normal P4 foglamp switch, mounted on the small auxiliary panel that sits next to the choke control; this would not look out of place and with the relays and extra wiring hidden behind the dash-panel, no-one would be any the wiser. This may not apply to 1950 "square instrument" models, with which I am not familiar. I should mention that the illustration above is for negative earth car; for a P4, which is positive earth the connections to terminals W1 and W2 would need to be reversed.

Incorporating indicator lamps

This is, perhaps, an easier problem to overcome, as cars of this period exported to U.S.A. were already fitted with flashing indicators, so all that is needed is to change the front and rear lamps to U.S. specification.

The front sidelamps need to be removed and replaced with twin-filament bulb holders, together with the more protruding lenses which allow for the larger 6/21 watt bulbs (1954 cars only need single filament bulb holders). The lamps, when installed, are very discreet; how many, for example, have noticed that OLT 399, featured on the front cover of "Rover P4, 1949-59" (Brooklands Books), published some years ago now, has these fitted?

As for the rear lamps, some cannabilism is called for! The bulb holder carrier incorporated in the assembly has space for two bulb holders, but on U.K. cars, only one is fitted. What is needed is to take a single filament lamp unit and remove the bulb holder from the flange plate by bending back the tags that secure it; this can then be refitted to the carrier by reversing the process, and finally soldering into position. Matt White has actually done this conversion on his own car, so he's probably the best person to advise.

Incorporating a warning lamp

This is a legal requirement. Whether or not you bother with it, is as they say, "In the hands of the operator"! Assuming you do wish to, there are not too many options.

The ignition warning lamp is impossible to use, due to the circuitry; similarly, the choke and oil pressure warning lamps are unsuitable as they have other switches to go through before they reach earth. The only one left is the main beam warning lamp, which would be fine until the main beam headlamps are needed; you would then have current feeding back into the flasher unit; also, the warning light circuit would try and flash the main beam headlamps in sympathy with the indicators, which I don't think would go down too well! What is needed, therefore, is a separate warning lamp, which leaves three alternatives; (a) fit a separate warning lamp on the dash panel, heater control panel or an auxiliary switch panel – functional, but wouldn't look right, (b) fit a U.S. specification speedo head, if available, which incorporates a warning lamp (pause for laughter), or (c) the best way, I think, and that is to replace the dash panel with a post-54 type, which already has a warning lamp fitted. You could always keep the original dash, should you want to reverse the process.

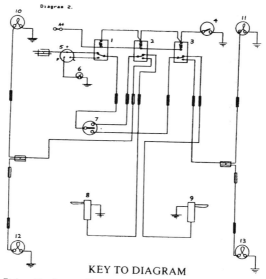

KEY TO DIAGRAM

1. Relay, Feed to traff. switch.
2. Relay, t/switch to ind., L.H.
3. Relay, t/switch to ind., R.H.
4. Switch
5. Flasher unit.
6. Warning lamp.
7. Trafficator switch.

8. Trafficator, L.H.
9. Trafficator, R.H.
10. Indicator, front L.H.
11. Indicator, front R.H.
12. Indicator, rear L.H.
13. Indicator, rear R.H.

High Intensity Sidelamps

I hit upon another idea while I was pondering over the indicator problem. Not only am I not the first one to think of it, however, but it doesn't conform to M.O.T. requirements, as Stan Johnstone found to his cost! I think it's a jolly good idea, anyway, and would be a definite advantage to those who use their P4's on a regular or daily basis. The modification applies to post-56 models and basically involves replacing the sidelamps with twin-filament units, as before. I thought of calling it High Intensity Sidelamps – HIS for short; I suppose you could call it High Energy Replacement Sidelamps, which would be HERS – but I digress. With the lamps on, the result would be very bright sidelamps OR normal sidelamps plus headlamps when driving, and normal sidelamps ONLY, when parked. The lamps would be much more visible than normal sidelamps (about the same as Volvo/Saab daylight running lights) and would really come into their own in poor light situations, like dusk, for example, but would draw less than half the current of headlamps. I am not suggesting that they are a substitute for headlamps however, when these are clearly needed. If anyone is interested in this conversion, I'd be pleased to go into further details; once again, relay and wiring modifications are involved and although, I think, it's a sensible and safety-conscious modification, it's not legal, and would need to be disconnected for the test.

Bryan Plummer   *July 1991*

RESEALING CALIPERS

I have received a number of calls recently from members having difficulty locating the retaining ring in the rubber boot when resealing calipers. When using a screwdriver to install the ring as recommended in the leaflet accompanying the seals, the ring tends to pop out one side whilst being pressed in the other causing much frustration.

I overcame this by making a disc from 16 gauge alloy of a diameter that would fit inside the retaining ring and the ring would not readily drop off. A short bolt was attached to the centre of the disc as a means of removing same when the retaining ring was finally in place.

Proceed as follows:-
1. Fit piston sealing ring in groove in caliper.
2. Lay caliper on its side.
3. Place ring on disc.
4. Insert disc and ring upwards into boot.
5. Lay boot over hole in caliper holding disc and ring clear.
6. Work boot into position with remaining fingers, followed by disc and ring – feeling through the upper side of boot.
7. When disc is centred, press home then remove disc leaving ring behind.
8. Check for correct fit.
9. Lubricate piston with Girling rubber grease or brake fluid and insert through boot.

Early pistons use the smaller ring to retain the boot in the piston groove – later pistons do not.

By the time you have fitted three boots, the fourth should go in at the first attempt.

Derek Humphreys

January 1992

ROVER '80'/WEBER SINGLE CHOKE CARB CONVERSION

The Weber takes a 'push on' petrol-pipe, so I have fitted 5ft of 'Gate 3225 Multi-fuel' ¼in universal fuel line and fitted in-line filter supplied with the Weber carb in place of the Rover blackplastic fuel line. (The filter should be fitted horizontally)

Now to Commence!

Remove the ball joint and bracket fitted to the new Weber butterfly shaft and RETAIN the ball and nut.

Remove the old Solex carb flexible shaft (item 46 on page 163 the Parts Book). Fit this to the Weber (it will fit O.K.).

Please Note

Due to the fact the new Weber carb butterfly shaft opens in the REVERSE direction to the old Solex you must now proceed as follows:-

Disconnect the 2 orange and 2 slate wires from the cam switches. Detach the cam switch assembly from the bulkhead by removing the three ⅝ x ¼ BSF bolts (don't drop them!).

Release the switch locknuts and unwind them to the ends of their threads. Give them a good clean with electrical switch cleaner and make sure they are working properly.

Remove the cam from its shaft (note which way it faces now, with the toe of the cam uppermost, as per fig C32 on page C.28 of Workshop Manual). Check condition of shaft and fit a new bearing (Fig 35, Page 163 Parts Book) if found to be worn.

Make up the conversion plate as per diagram and fit the new Weber ball joint as indicated in diagram No. 1.

The old Rover ball joint is no longer required, but do not cut it off as it acts as a retainer for the conversion plate (see diagram 1).

Drill the pivot shaft bracket and fit a new ½in x ³⁄₁₆in bolt, SPRING-washer

93

and bolt as indicated on the conversion plate. NOTE: This plate MUST be secure.

Rotate the pivot shaft (item 23, Parts Book) 180° from its original 'at rest' position so that the ball joints now face the engine valve cover.

REVERSE the cam on its shaft rotate it 90° so that the slot now faces UPPERMOST with the locking bolt horizontal. (You may need to reverse the direction of the 1¼ x 2BA bolt to assist tightening finally).

Tighten the cam as indicated and adjust the switch clearance as per Workshop Manual, but remember, THEY ARE NOW WORKING IN REVERSE.

Fit the cam/switch bracket back on the bulkhead and correctly align the Weber carb shaft and pivot shaft assembly for COMPLETE FREEDOM OF MOVEMENT. Tighten all bolts gently.

Reverse the throttle lever (Fig 28 Parts Book) on its cross shaft, so the ball now faces the cylinder block.

SOLEX/WEBER CONVERSION

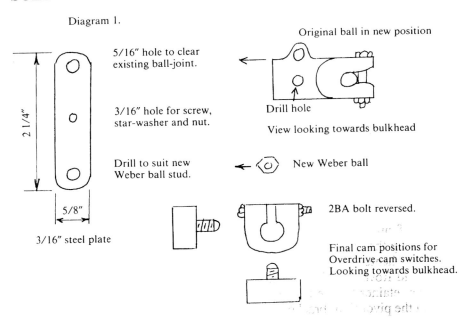

Diagram 1.

Deterioration of the underbody

Abrasion by stones will damage the original protection; the resultant surface rusting sweats away concealed by the accumulation of moisture retaining road silt. Winter salt can also be harboured in these death dealing poultices. The corrosion eventually eats through the underbody to the coachwork.

The original underbody protection was only adequate; early cars seem to be finished with primer and chassis black. Later cars may have this supplemented by factory applied underseal. The actual chassis of the vehicles seems only to have been covered in one coat of chassis black. Since these protective layers suffer much abrasive damage, deteriorate with age, and were seldom, if ever, cleaned, it is not surprising that most outwardly shiny P4's have rusty underbodies.

Beneath the front wings

The front valance panel; this runs between the front wings, below the bumper. The construction of the joints permits water retention by capillary action and in extreme cases may appear holed.

Under the wing, mud accumulates on the ledge below the headlamp bowls, which the valance and front apron are bolted to. In extreme cases, the base of the front wings rot through, especially by the bottom corners of the radiator grille. Damage may also extend to the inner wing and base of the radiator support frame. This area is fed with water from the bonnet drainage channel drain holes.

Mud collecting around the headlamp bowls will eventually rot them through. This leads to a deterioration in headlamp reflector silvering and perforation allows condensation to form within the headlamps..... (brings tears to my eyes!). Water may also penetrate behind the seal between the headlamp and the front wing leading to lacey edges around the headlamps mounting area.

Mud may accumulate above the headlamps leading to holes through the wing on pre-'57 cars.

Post '57 vehicles, with the indicator at the top of the wing, suffer silt accumulation which initially rots through above the lamp and thereafter all round it.

Mud may also collect around the front wheel arch lip leading to frayed edges and holes through the swage line. However the main weakness, without exception, is the rear of the front wheel arch where the wing is sealed to the bulkhead. Corrosion travels along the base of the bulkhead in the general direction of the front door, weakening the whole area behind it. Why? The gap between the bulkhead and the front wing is sealed by a rubber strip attached to a metal J-shaped securing plate and fixed to the bulkhead with set screws. The rubber strip is compressed against the bulkhead to form a seal and at right angles pressed against the inside surface of the front wing. Thus there are several layers of material for water to seep behind, and once the metal J-strip corrodes through (from the bottom upwards), filth can more easily penetrate the void behind. Thereafter the rot eats the base of the bulkhead and the wing behind the stainless moulding. A line of corrosion may be apparent outside above the moulding and up the wing in line with the rubber seal. Corrosion may progress into the door hinge mounting and also beneath the sill rubbers..... eventually weakness may develop in the base of the B/C post. The wheel arch lip is usually less badly affected except at the bottom corner, by the rubber strip, which stays damp longer because that's where the water drains.

Immediately above the J-shaped rubber strip is a piece of sponge designed to stop large amounts of road dirt entering the engine bay. Eventually this rubber saturates and prolonged contact between steel and damp rubber leads to corrosion, water then appears to be fed into and along the spot welded join between the front and inner wing panels causing severe rust induced swelling in extreme cases.

The Chassis

Mud can accumulate on the top surface of the chassis beneath the front inner wings, particularly between the bolts securing the steering idler (see Overdrive 43, 13), the chassis may even be perforated. (The steering box side seems to benefit from slight oil seepage) Dirt and small stones may also collect at the bottom of the road springs and annoy the steel base plate.

The jacking point supports are weakened by exposure to the high velocity fire of road filth spraying at them from the front wheels – as is the handbrake mechanism protection box. Corrosion may be sufficient to cause these items to break away and rot may nibble the floor around the handbrake detectable inside the vehicle. Contributions to this latter also come from a failed bulkhead area.

The two main chassis members running under the car are usually acceptable; due in part to the covering of oil received from a leaky rear main oil seal via the bell housing base. However the chassis outriggers, (extensions supporting the jacking points and body mountings bolted to the sills) are more exposed and may be eaten away if filth has built up in them.

At the rear of the car, the sides of the chassis are exposed to abrasion from road dirt in the rear wheel arch, the petrol pipe on the top surface may become fragile and the rear axle bumpstop rubbers may drop off when rust penetrates their mounting. The rear body mounting support channel may become weakened to the extent that the rear body is not located to the chassis!

Lastly, spray may consume the spare wheel tray and the inside of the spare wheel door with surface rust; however these items may clean up satisfactorily. The battery box is more likely to be nibbled by escaping acid than rust.

Rear Wheel arches

Construction of the wheel arch lip is more complex than at the front; the inner wheel arch is spot welded all the way round to the outer wing. Water penetrating the join will cause the lip to swell; accumulated mud on the lip will preferentially attack the spot welds (weld material is always more susceptible to rust attack) and rust may break through the coachwork in a line around the arch, especially behind the D post. Here mud collects, travelling up the wheel arch from the bolt securing the stainless moulding; the inner arch may become perforated so allowing water into the rear door hinge area and beneath those sill mats once more; the lip by the moulding may disintegrate. If the inner arch gets perforated further forward, then corrosion will break through the coachwork down the D post – but this is extreme. The inner surface of the inner wheel arch may rot around the boot hinge mountings (boot refuses to stay up). Other holes may permit water to enter the car interior (found beneath the rear seat cushion) and the boot etc.

Splash plates fitted in the rear valance do a good job of preventing muck from rotting out the spare wheel door hinge supports; but they are usually sacrificed in the process and eventually holes appear by them in the valences. Absence of the splash plate also provides less support for the spare wheel door hinges which are then prone to seize – thereafter corrosion and excessive leverage on the door will cause the hinges to break away. In certain cases it is not unusual to find little correct coachwork on a P4 beneath the rear bumper line. The boot floor corners (above the splash plates) are also prone to disappear – particularly on the petrol pump side (not '80' models), water is then able to enter the boot, and escape this time, but the damage has already been done.

Summing Up

This may all sound depressing but merely serves to illustrate the downhill path; fortunately little of the above will put a car off the road. The areas of interest to an M.O.T. inspector are the security and condition of the lamps and likewise for the body mounting points; otherwise structural integrity is maintained by the chassis. However, perhaps it will be your own inability to continue with a suffering, sad looking vehicle in the long term which sorely taxes your staying power, even when road-worthiness is not the issue.

This list is only a guide based on my experience; corrections to both errors and ignorance would be appreciated.

Paul Hart   *1987 Yearbook*

CLUTCH SPINDLE OVERHAUL

With regards to the recent "Overdrive" bulletin, I thought that you might like to know about my recent experiences with Rover spares.

Firstly, the Windsor Motor Company of Sheet Street, Windsor, have been having a stores clear-out and recently had on display a brand-new distributor for a Rover '75', and a brand-new windscreen wiper motor for a Rover '90'. (This I believe, fits quite a lot of the P4 range). They also had some rear number-plate brackets, also brand-new, at £1.00 each.

Over the past several months the clutch on my Rover '100' has been becoming increasingly stiff in operation, being due, I thought, to wear in the bronze-type bush which connects the clutch pedal spindle unit to the gear-box casing. These bushes are very easy to replace once you have got your car over a pit or on a hoist, and are still available, I am informed by a Rover dealer's storesman, at 15 pence each plus V.A.T. This is what I paid. The current part number is: 217984. They are also available from a dealer in 'Lewisham' who has had some bushes specially made, and they come with two small sandwich plates that go on either side. They sell these at £4.00 each plus 20 pence postage.

Now back to my clutch..... I found that the actual clutch spindle, which is located through the main chassis member, was almost completely seized. It can be seen from the Workshop Manual that the brake pedal is located on the off-side end of this and pivots freely on the end, retained by a small bolt. The whole clutch linkage and brake pedal should be, and was, removed allowing access and a judicious tapping with a hammer to knock the clutch spindle out. I found it had not seen much lubricant for some time, and was partially rusty. A good clean with emery paper and plenty of grease meant that on re-assembly, the clutch works beautifully.

This is quite a straight-forward job and certainly makes a great difference to the feel of the car. As with any car maintenance, a good look at the Workshop Manual is essential before starting this job, and then it all makes sense! Incidentally, I have not seen any particular reference to routine lubrication of the offending clutch spindle, and it could quite easily be missed. A good dousing with oil every few months should do the trick.

I hope that my experience may be of help to others

Keep up the good Rover work

Andrew H. Shaw

1988 Yearbook

SYNTHETIC ENGINE OILS?

No one seems to have objected to my putting SAAB SAE 75 oil into my gearbox, so how about a synthetic oil for the engine?

Don't get me wrong, modern oils like Castrol GTX and Duckhams are very good – but give them the finger and thumb test after a year and 5,000 miles and there is a noticeable decrease in slipperiness.

I first tried synthetic oil in a VW Golf five years ago: that car has now done over 100,000. My 120,000 mile SAAB Turbo has always had synthetic: it still runs like new. Our Morris 1300 (66,000) and Morris Ital (120,000) run noticeably better with synthetic, so why not my 1955 '90' at only 110,000?

I knew my engine was clean inside, since I had dredged at least ¼" of gunge off the bottom of the sump last year. Previously I had run some highly detergent diesel oil through the engine for a week – that had certainly shifted the muck.

Auntie has some high-friction areas – the camshaft in particular – surely synthetic can't do any harm, except to the bank balance? So in January, 8 litres of Mobil 1 was installed and as a result the engine starts easier and runs noticeably smoother and freer. Oil consumption appears unchanged at 200 to the pint as always but I appear to have 'lost' about 5 psi oil pressure when hot and I can hear that rumbling main bearing slightly more – it will need attention shortly!! Suppose I shouldn't grumble after 37 years?

All very well having an oil gauge, but, rather like a heart monitor, one soon becomes a hypochondriac . . . but where *did* that 5 psi go? Lurking deep in the engine compartment is the oil pressure relief valve – adjustable on early cars, fixed on roller-cam models – but after 37 years the spring was unable to maintain even 40 psi when hot. I could, of course, screw it all the way on and jam the ball on the seating, but the cold pressure would then be astronomical.

I invested in a new spring: it was longer and stronger than the old one and the 'hot' pressure shot up to 50 psi whilst the 'cold' pressure remained at a reasonable 65 psi. If anyone is interested, I took a set of measurements for comparison purposes . . .

In April it was colder than January! As I write in May it is roasting – I see no reason to change my conclusions that synthetic oil has been an improvement, and they reckon it can stay in for 25,000 miles so it should work out quite a bit cheaper in the long run. Whether it is worth the initial £40 investment I shall leave up to you.

Jim Butterworth   *September 1992*

ROVER '60' VYR 720 (ALIAS AUNTIE VERA)

Having owned Auntie now for just over two years, I thought I should put pen to paper about a persistent problem I've had with big end knock on acceleration, coming in just prior to gear change rev band. As this was now to be my everyday car (all this came about, I'm happy to say, when the wife's Allegro needed a new engine and we were looking around for a Rover 213, the same as I was running, when she happened to say: "You've always wanted another P4 like we used to have 20 odd years ago". This was also a '60', a nice black 1956 with old type wings and high boot and wrap around window. I still like that shape. (Anyone out there got my old '60' SLK 967? I would like to hear from you) Well I mean fancy the wife waving a red flag to a bull. You get no points for guessing what car she is now running! I retarded the ignition slightly and drove cautiously for some 14 months before I had time to strip and rebuild the engine. Funny thing was even though it was a big end knock the symptoms were opposite, i.e. labour it on hill it would go quiet as a mouse and any speed over 50 it was OK. It also had a good oil pressure at tick-over when hot.

Eventually I did a complete strip down only to find nothing was worn more than 0.0008 thou (which just goes to show how well built these engines are after 34 years). Despair set in as it was expensive to strip out the crankshaft, as new shells and seals were fitted back. I do not believe in using old ones once disturbed. Anyway it had a good decoke, valves ground in, hydraulic tensioner overhaul, new jet and needle in carburettor, plugs, points, leads, condenser, water pump overhaul and new hoses.

The engine appears to be in good condition as it only uses ¾ pint of oil between services. I do this at 4,000 miles and change the filter every time.

So back to the problem of big end knock. The only thing that can cause timing problems must be associated with the distributor. So a letter to Stan Johnstone explaining the problem and could he give me any information on the correct distributor, vacuum unit, springs, etc. Stan kindly wrote back giving me the correct spring part number and Lucas Technical Information Dept address. Many thanks, Stan, for your interest and information. So a letter off to Lucas with all the details from the distributor and vacuum unit. Lucas's Mr Davenport, Customer Technical Services, was very helpful.

The following information may be of help to others.
Type DMBZ4A 404 10D 6113   10.58
Vacuum 419681   4-18-12
4 = is inches of mercury at which advancement begins
18 = is inches of mercury at which advancement ends
12 = is maximum advance in distributor degrees

The cam inside the distributor body can be assembled 180° apart. One side is marked 13, the other 25. The former is to go against the stop.

The springs are LU410605, both the same, and consist of the following: 5½ turns of 0.026" SWG wire outside dia 0.192", overall length including loops 0.705" – all this exciting information and guess what? All was correct. I even marked the flywheel in degrees and checked with a strobe the vacuum unit. You've guessed, it was correct. I was by now getting exasperated – it has got to be the springs. Yes, they were very shiny for 30 odd year old springs, but did they measure up correctly. Perhaps they are new, but of a softer spring steel. So I took the bull by the horns and took one out and replaced it with a homemade one of thicker gauge. To my amazement it cured the problem and it was advancing fully.

This was left like this until I came to do another service of points and condenser. Whilst undertaking this (fate I suppose) I dropped the unit holding the the wires and spring contact into the distributor body. Whilst retrieving the nut, having removed the base plate to facilitate, my old problem loomed up before me. Why had I not noticed this before? The fixed posts supporting the springs were bent inwards slightly. I immediately bent them to 90°, replaced my homemade spring with the original. *Problem cured.* I can only assume a previous owner or garage mechanic had fitted new springs and bent the posts in to get them on (as they are strong) but not enough to make the rotor arm sloppy in the static position. So all you P4 owners, before condemning the engine to the scrap heap or think of buying a new distributor, *CHECK YOUR POSTS!!*

Mike Coleman
September 1992

REAR WINDOW REPAIRS

I have recently had the rear window frame of my '100' rechromed and have renewed the rubber seal so I thought members might be interested in this operation.

The Workshop Manual details how to remove the window from the car. However, when all the clips were removed, it needed levering from inside with a tyre lever to unstick it from the body and two helpers outside to catch it.

Clean the old sealer from the frame and remove the old rubber seal. I found the best way to do this was to cut down each side of the seal with a Stanley knife, after which it comes out in three pieces. Remove the countersunk screws from each side of the frame and after a considerable amount of pulling, the frame will come away from the glass. A thin blade can be a help here to unstick the glazing rubber. New glazing rubber will be required and I used a channel section, catalogue No. R315 from Woolies of Market Deeping.

The Works Manual again explains how to fit the glass into the frame which was fairly straightforward. However, I was unable to close up the two sections of the frame to insert the screws in spite of using cord loops tightened with lengths of dowel to pull them together. I therefore retired to the local windscreen fitting depot where it took four of us two hours to persuade the frame to close. The rubber seal is then pressed into the frame with the aid of soap solution and a screwdriver.

Not having the clamps shown in the Workshop Manual to pull the unit to the body, I laid it over the aperture and then connected a set of pulleys to the centre bottom of the frame with the other end anchored to the hole in the transmission cover through which the gear box is filled. This enabled the bottom of the frame to be pulled in and a pair of clips loosely fitted to the bottom edge. The pulleys were then transferred to the top and clip fitting continued around the screen with the additional aid of a tyre lever to pull the frame in close to the body.

Screws can be finally tightened when you are happy with the alignment. Two lengths of self tapping screws are used and care needs to be taken to ensure that the correct length screw is used in each hole so as not to foul the outer skin.

Shims are also fitted under some clips but they do not necessarily go back in the same position when a new rubber is fitted and additional shims may be required. Do not use the screws to pull the frame into place – lever the frame then tighten the screws.

I did not use any sealant between frame and body before fitting but subsequently injected sealer under the rubber.

In hindsight, it may have been the pre-formed rubber channel which caused the difficulties in closing the frame, perhaps the flat rubber glazing strip, 2" x ¹⁄₁₆" – 11' required, which Woolies also sell, would have been better as this is of slightly thinner section.

My final advice is that unless things are extremely desperate, leave well alone.

D. Humphreys

March 1993

S.U. FUEL PUMPS

On repairing a S.U. fuel pump recently, I found that I couldn't get it to run properly. I then remembered (terrible memory these days!) that about three years ago, a batch of contacts were made with the "roll-over" springs just too long, making it difficult for the points to trip over without the springs getting stuck under the 'cage'.

I won't mention the company, but the contact set is sold in a small blue and yellow box. I think you know the ones I mean.

If you have removed a set of contacts that have just burnt out, but have been working well, you can very carefully remove the offending springs from them and place them in the new cage, with gentle use of a pair of long nosed pliers, but I wouldn't really recommend this unless you are desperate. Ideally only use S.U. points in the plastic bag. Single pumps were SU AUA 6021 and double ones SU AUB 6022.

Don't forget to bleed the pump of air on fitting by 'cracking' the outlet pipe with the ignition on, allowing the air to escape and then a steady stream of petrol.

If after doing this, the pump is still rattling away, you very likely have a tiny hole in the inlet pipe, which will have to be renewed.

Stan Johnstone   ***March 1993***

CHANGED EARTH POLARITY

From the early 1930's onwards British cars were all built with what is known as positive earth, that is, the positive side of the battery is connected to the car chassis to form the return path for all the electrical systems on the car. The Volkswagen Beetle was for many years the exception to this rule on British roads. Not only did the early Beetles have a 6 volt electrical system but also they were wired negative earth. There is no clear reason why any manufacturer adopted one or the other of these systems. It has been argued that one or the other is better from the corrosion point of view, but as far as I am aware there is little or no supporting evidence.

What is a clear technical advantage is if everyone adopts the same standard, and here we have had to fall into line with other countries. The standard is now negative earth, and it looks as if that is fixed for all time. In past years the earth polarity of a car had little significance other than remembering which way round to put in the battery if it were taken out. Now, however, with the proliferation of polarity-sensitive electronic equipment, it is imperative to ensure that the polarity of the car matches any equipment you may want to install in it.

The usual reason, therefore, for wanting to change round the earth polarity is to fit a modern radio or car alarm, all of which are made to work negative earth – in fact this has been standardised for so long that many pieces of equipment no longer have a polarity warning in their instructions.

Radios made up to the early seventies were often made dual polarity and if you want to fit a radio to a positive earth car it may be worth looking around for one which can be made to fit the car. Sometimes there is an external plug which can be reversed, or there may be soldered connections to turn round inside.

P2, P3, P4, 3 litre Mark I and II and early P6 were positive earth. As it is normally the P4 that I am asked to change, I have listed below all the points that must be attended to on a P4. Other models will differ only in detail.

1. The Battery: The same battery may be used, but the connections to it will have to be reversed. The terminals are normally towards the offside; turn the battery round so that they are towards the centre of the car. The main battery lead will have to have its terminal changed to the larger positive type; if the car already has the clamp type terminals they can be changed over. The main lead should be long enough to reach across the battery tray. If it is not, there will be spare length further forward which can be worked back through the clips on the chassis. The earth lead will need replacing with a longer one, as well as having its terminal changed. It is fastened to a lug on the chassis just behind the battery tray.

2. The ammeter: This has two terminals, and all the wires from one should be transferred to the other, and vice versa. If this is not done it will read in reverse. This part is best done whilst the battery is disconnected.

3. The screenwasher: On a '110' an electric screenwasher was fitted as standard, and many other P4's have had electric washers fitted. The wires to the motor should be reversed. Some screenwasher pumps will pump less efficiently if they rotate backwards; others will actually pump backwards.

4. The coil: The coil as fitted had one terminal marked 'SW' for 'switch' and one marked 'CB' for 'contact breaker'. The connections to this should be reversed. Later coils are marked '+' and '−'; for the negative earth the '−' should be connected to the contact breaker.

5. The dynamo: A dynamo is capable of charging a battery either way round without any wiring alterations. The only factor that determines which way round it will 'wake up' as the engine turns is the small amount of remanent magnetism left in the dynamo yoke from the last time it was energised. I have always found that the safest way to repolarise the dynamo is to first change round the battery, then disconnect the wire from the 'F' terminal on the regulator. Touch this wire five or six times on to the 'A' or 'B' terminal; there will be a small spark produced. Reconnect it to the 'F' terminal – the dynamo is now repolarised. An alternator, incidentally, cannot be changed in this way, as it contains diodes which are set one way round.

6. The radio: If the car already has a radio installed, it must either be changed round or disconnected.

7. The fuel pump: If you purchase a new SU fuel pump, or indeed, if you take one of my rebuilt ones, it will come with a diode to suppress the spark at the contacts instead of the capacitor which was originally used. A diode suppressor will make the contacts last longer, but it then renders the pump polarity sensitive. Any pump with a diode in it should be marked as 'positive earth' or 'negative earth'. If your pump is not marked then you need do nothing with it as it will have a capacitor in it. If it has a diode in it, the diode must be reversed or the pump will not function.

8. Anything else? Look round the car to see if anything else has been fitted which could be polarity sensitive. A built in charger, perhaps, or a charger plug? An alarm? If there is, it must be attended to.

9. Labels: It is a good idea to label the car as negative earth, both by the battery and under the bonnet, for the benefit of anyone else who may be working on it. I was once nearly caught out by a car which was negative earth but not labelled as such.

After all is done, start the engine and check that the charging system is operating correctly. Then fit your new radio!

John Backhouse   *January 1994*

MORE INSIDE LOCKING ADVICE!

Paul Toth seeks advice on converting his driver's door handle to lock from the inside. As I've just completed the exercise, perhaps a few words may help.

The task could not be simpler, no modifications are necessary, only the removal of a small screw identified from the parts lists as "special drive screw 78111". When the trim is removed – as all the best manuals say, glossing over the problems involved – you find the part of the door latch mechanism which carries the interior handle is held on by three screws. Carefully removing these and moving the mechanism to the right exposes the screw in the face of the latch mechanism. It's quite easy to remove and reassembly (as the manual always says) is in reverse order. The parts list shows that whether a left hand drive or right hand drive car, the locking handle was always on the right hand door so those overseas don't need to modify these instructions!

Of course there is a snag and I've experienced it! We all know that P4's were built with everything organised for a purpose, so the drive screw wasn't there by accident.

This modification allows you to lock yourself in – but it also allows you to lock yourself out! The outer lock doesn't interact so locking the driver's door from the inside and closing it gives absolute security. A bent letter opener and a steel rule should be carried in the boot for use in emergencies for tweaking the quarterlight open – enclose a S.A.E. for sketch! Then you can reach in and open the door from the inside. I will keep the modification as there have been times when I or my wife wished we could lock the driver door – but the entry kit stays in the boot.

Ian P. Harris

November 1992

DISTRIBUTING THE SPARK

Many of our P4's are still operating with the original distributor as fitted in the Rover factory on their initial build and, of course, their mileage accumulation may be great or relatively small. If the spindle of the unit has been given a small, but regular shot of lubrication throughout its life, it may well be performing a good job of supplying a steady impetus for the engine's ignition to function satisfactorily.

However, in view of the amount of calls I get concerning various ignition problems, I thought I would jot a few notes down to help clear a few points (no pun intended!).

Firstly, on the mechanical side of the distributor, there are only a few components that are prone to wear, these being: the main spindle and bush (on earlier models, a ball race bearing is incorporated and can develop wear after high mileages, especially with neglect on maintaining lubrication). Slight wear can occur on the top spindle integral with the cam-lobes and balance weight anchors. Obviously, any wear in the aforementioned parts will give way to intermittent opening of the contact points, because the cam-lobes are not revolving true to the axis of the spindle. This fluctuation can usually be seen when a strobe light is used to check the ignition timing. If you make a thorough job of cleaning the timing marks on the flywheel and then carefully paint the 'before-top-dead-centre' timing line that is correct for your particular model with either white enamel or the typist's friend –Tippex – you will then see the marks very clearly with the engine running and the strobe is flashing at the No. 1 firing point. With the engine running at tick-over, the timing mark should stay devoted to the marks. Any fluctuation from either side of the line will show the amount of wear that is present. At this stage, you can increase the revs of the engine and check that the advance/retard mechanism is working correctly, i.e. the timing mark should promptly disappear out of the fly-wheel cover aperture or window. If the line stays stubbornly where it is, it either means that the diaphragm is ruptured in the advance/retard housing, or that the balance weights or springs are not functioning as they should. The diaphragm can be checked by sucking on the end of its chamber after removing the capillary pipe attached to it and observing whether the swivel lever is moving inwards towards the chamber. These are rare beasts to find, but I should think Geoffrey Kent will be able to supply you with an excellent replacement.

The little advance/retard springs can become fatigued and stretched on high mileage P4's but I often find that they have been damaged on a previous overhaul by the use of pliers to unhook them from their posts. The only way to remove them is with a strong squeeze between finger and thumb! That way, you will not distort the spring in any way.

These springs vary from model to model, because their torsion works in conjunction with the balance weights. Again these Lucas springs are hard to locate these days.

By and large, the most common fault is wear in the main spindle and bush. Unless you are an engineer and have access to machine-shop facilities, this is not a job you can tackle yourself as it involves dismantling the distributor completely and making a new bush. When I repair distributors, I make the new bush from phosphor bronze as this has a very high resistance to wear and also, of course, is much more suited to the job than the sintered cast metal used in the original mass produced item. Phosphor bronze would have been prohibitive for a high production run. If you are able to renovate your own distributor, be careful not to make the bush – which has two outside diameters – too tight a fit in the body of the distributor. A maximum of .0005" (.0127mm) interference fit is necessary and even then, the bush should be fitted cold from the freezer and the distributor body hot from being dunked in a pan of boiling water for five minutes. Trying to fit the bush without this preparatory precaution, could result in cracking the unit. Once the bush is fitted, you then carefully hone the bush to give a total working clearance of .0004" (.010mm). After honing very meticulously, clean the bush and spindle before lubricating and re-assembling. Do not forget to drill a new oil hole in the bush!

If you cannot do this rather specialised work yourself, you will either have to look around for a used distributor which has fared rather better than yours, or go to someone like Holden who can supply you with a rebuilt unit.

Really worn distributors can produce quite an awful rattling sound whereby the vibrations can be felt by grasping the distributor cap whilst the engine is running.

If the valves and their seats are in good order along with the ignition leads, plugs and covers and, of course, the carburation and distributor are in tip-top condition, this can really be the icing on the cake for a super smooth P4 engine.

A steady contact breaker gap is important for the ignition coil to do its job to the full too, as the dwell angle (the number of degrees the points are closed during one ignition cycle) determines the length of time available for primary current to build up in the coil, and therefore produce the strongest possible spark. Couple this with a good condenser and you are in business, provided, of course, the contact breaker gap is set correctly along with the ignition timing. As I have said before, the points gap can be set quite adequately using feeler gauges, but if you have got the use of a dwell meter, all the better for spot on settings. The dwell angles for the P4's are $38° \pm 3°$ for all six cylinder engines except the '110' which is $35° \pm 3°$ and $60° \pm 3°$ for the four cylinder '60's and '80's. Do not forget to lubricate the steady post and cam lobes on fitting new points to the distributor.

Another cause for ignition problems which can be annoyingly intermittent, is the break-down of the tiny low tension wire which is attached, but insulated, to the inside of the distributor body feeding through from the low tension wire attaches to the outside of the body. This very important little piece of wire attached, along with the condenser wire, to the moving arm of the points is made up of many very fine wires. The original wire used was cotton covered and over the years literally falls to pieces. If you go into an electronic spares shop like RS or Maplin and explain the type of wire you require, they will be happy to sell you a modern plastic covered equivalent which will make an excellent replacement for this often troublesome piece of wire. If you then carefully remove the tags from the old wire, using a soldering iron, you can make up a new replacement by soldering the tags to the wire ends.

If the contact points appear to burn and become pitted after a relatively short mileage and look 'sooty' around the contacts, this is almost certainly due to a badly functioning condenser. This cannot be tested for faults and should just be replaced with a new one. The surface faces of the contacts are very finely coated with a hard layer of metal to prevent oxidation taking place and frequent cleaning will soon wear through this coating and cause mis-firing. So do not clean them too frequently.

Quite a common problem with the P4 ignition system is the fact that very often rain can enter through the join down the middle of the bonnet – underneath the trim strip – and create corrosion in the plug lead ends and around the spark plugs. Careful cleaning of the lead ends with a fine wire brush should get the sparks at full strength again.

A persistent mis-firing can sometimes be caused by the suppressors fitted between the leads and the spark plug covers. The late '95' and '110' were fitted with suppressed leads in place of separate suppressors and can also break down causing intermittent firing. If your car is fitted with suppressors and you cannot detect an ignition problem, simply remove them from the leads and run the engine without them. If the car runs smooth under all driving conditions, you will then know the culprit.

One last thing to check is the low tension between the CB terminal on the coil to the terminal on the side of the distributor. This lead can sometimes break down, particularly if it hasn't been replaced over many years of service.

Sometimes a 'cracking' sound can be heard when the engine is pulling hard. This is usually due to a split in one or more of the spark plug covers, causing the spark to arc across to the cylinder head. The best check for this condition, is to run the engine in a dark garage whereby you might well witness quite a 'firework' display!

THE ROVER *95*

THE ROVER *100*

THE ROVER *105R*

THE ROVER *110*

If, after cleaning and gapping the spark plugs – or better still replacing them – your engine is still running unevenly, you will then have to forget the ignition and carry out a compression test on each cylinder to determine whether you have burnt out a valve. More about that in a future article.

Stan Johnstone

March 1994

SWIVEL PINS, BUSHES AND COTTER-PINS

You will have read in Matt's editorial, this edition, that I had experienced problems with his swivel pin bushes and cotter-pins.

Matt had spotted a full set (both sides) of swivel pins, bushes, ball-race, seals and cotter-pins on the auto-jumble stand at NEC and asked me to inspect them before he bought them.

I went along to the stand to have a look and, to be quite honest, was only concerned that the swivel pins were correct and properly ground with the right number of splines to suit the top-anchor. Some were made a few years ago with one spline too many would you believe?

All the parts were in Leyland boxes and the pins were in first class condition. I didn't even think to look at the rest of the parts. Silly me!

Once Matt had given me both radius arms and stub axles, I got to work on replacing the pins and bushes. To my horror, I opened the bags with the bushes in. I couldn't believe my eyes. The bushes had been so-called turned by someone I can only describe as an animal. They had been squeezed so tightly in the chuck jaws of the lathe, that the seal counterbores were like old three-penny bits. No way would the seals have entered these bores, let alone remained round to seal round the pin.

Not only that, but the outside diameter of the bushes was at least .004 thou/inch oversize making them far too tight for fitting into their housings in the stub-axle.

To top it all, the bores of the bushes were minus .010 to .014 thou/inch which is far too much for a reamer to contend with.

The only saving grace, of course, was the fact that they were in a 'metal-on' condition and I was able to re-machine them prior to fitting.

That done, I proceeded with the build-up after reaming the bushes in-situ using the Guild's adjustable reamers. With the pin fitting nicely, I started to fit the cotter-pins only to discover that they were of the later ⁵⁄₁₆" thread type (which is no problem) but after a bit of a struggle, I measured them to find that they were 10mm diameter and not the ⅜" (.375 inch) they should have been.

So the job became a nightmare rather that the pleasant task it should have been. So beware – there are some cowboys about! They caught me out, so be careful when buying from NON-ROVER partsmen at auto-jumbles.

The only good thing about the whole affair was the fact that I didn't get Matt's '90' ready for the Norwich Union run and had to use my '95'. I did enjoy myself going round Silverstone, even though it cost me about three months tyre wear in one day!

Stan Johnstone   *July 1994*

DID YOU KNOW…?

… That all is not lost if you lose the number of the key which fits boot and glovebox on a P4. On the '95' and '110' the number is stamped on the plate which can be seen by opening the passenger front door, but on earlier models it is stamped on the top of the radiator. The number is on the left hand end of the radiator, and should be read by standing to the side of the car. There will be three digits, roughly ⅜" high. The two letters which precede the number (FP, FS, FK, FR) can be found by trying other keys in the lock, as the letters define the shape of the flutes cut into the side of the key. There may also be a check here with the numbers, as not every number combination was available with each letter group. There was a time when the local accessory shop would have several cards on the wall and could select a key when quoted the number. Now, however, these cards are held by the specialist suppliers who have to be approached either by post or at autojumbles.

… That on all P4's except the Cyclops the petrol pick-up pipe is well over to the right hand side of the petrol tank. This little snippet may be of no great interest, you may think, but it is of significance if you have already covered some miles switched on to reserve and are desperately looking for a filling station. The general advice is to stay on the crown of the road as much as possible, for if you stay on a nearside camber for too long the pump will suck air and the engine will cut out. I once watched someone who ran out of petrol and parked on a nearside camber. He fetched a gallon of petrol in a can and poured it into the tank. The car would still not start until it was pushed into the centre of the road – and a P4 is no light weight!

All the other Rover cars around this period – late P2, P3, Cyclops, P5 – have their pick-up in the centre of the tank and do not suffer the problem. With the late P4 it seems that there was a competition for space with the spare wheel tray which forced the pick-up on to one side, and the right hand side was chosen so that the pump would not have to compete for space with the filler neck.

... That on all the P4's which have an oil bath air cleaner, removal is much easier that a lot of people think. The air cleaner has to come off for a number of jobs, including changing the fan belt. The workshop manual instructs to "Unscrew the air cleaner" which does not give much away, and the novice can easily spend a knuckle-scraping hour undoing the long bolt directly under the air cleaner, and the small one bracing it to the dynamo bracket. Once you know, however, removal could hardly be simpler. All you have to do is turn the whole air cleaner anti-clockwise and it will unscrew itself from a bolt welded on to the bracket. On the very early models the bolt is loose and must be held from underneath. Many a time I have removed the air cleaner from a customer's car to hear an exclamation of 'I wish I'd known that a week ago!'

Jon Backhouse

September 1994

CARB SWAP FOR A ROVER '80'

We've had VVY 444 for about 5 years now, and although she's got just 33,000 miles on the clock, the old girl did occasionally (well, to be truthful, every time the loud pedal was pressed actually) show signs of breathing difficulty, thanks to Mr Solex and his petroleum spirit vaporising instrument.

444 also had another habit when hot, in that each time the engine was stopped, a float bowl full of 4 star skilfully crept out of its allotted receptacle,

and via the choke tube and throttle spindle, make like a Lemming onto the manifold.

Now, in spite of being a Yorkshireman (with a bit of Dane mixed in) I have not calculated the value of the lost fuel, but did notice the exorbitant price of a replacement starter motor. This was of some relevance, as the excesses of BP's finest that came to rest in the inlet manifold, meant that this almost priceless article, had to work overtime, spinning the flywheel until 2286cc took over. I had thought about leaving the car in gear during this procedure in order that some of the time could be spent travelling.

So, the threat of needless expense, along with the soot-fall from the exhaust when she did fire up (which incidentally, I found slightly embarrassing, as folk were beginning to confuse my car with Wheater's) prompted some investigations.

Overhauling the Solex failed to solve the problem of flooding when hot, which was my main concern, as to be fair, 444 always started instantly when cold and managed 30 - 32 mpg with ease. The flat spots, which come as standard with the Solex, at light throttle openings, I could live with.

Back issues of Overdrive suggested various alternative carbs., but I could find no mention of a fairly obvious replacement – a Zenith 361V.

As most of you will know, the P4 '80' shares the same underbonnet accessory as that of the farmer's favourite, the Land Rover. A few enquiries soon revealed that the Agriculture impecunious had also got cheesed off with the Solex, so Land Rover had recommended the Zenith as the alternative.

A trip to the local 4WD shop led to a brand new carb and cast adaptor plate, which allows the Zenith to be turned through 90°, finding its way into my hands. A bendy friend helped to take the sting out of the bill for £98, and off we went.

Closer examination revealed only one small hitch in the fitting process. Solex spindle rotates clockwise, Zenith anti-clockwise. It soon became apparent that the simple expedient of turning the carb pivot shaft through 180°, and fitting the control rod at the other side of the shaft wouldn't work. The subsequent ministrations of a hacksaw and welding torch resulted in the lug holding the pivot ball being transplanted to the other side of the shaft – success! Everything fitted and turned as it should. Pipe work was replaced, which left only the choke cable to sort out. The original was about 4" too short as it now had to bend through 90° to meet the mechanism. Wanting to retain the original outer cable I pondered and rummaged, and found a spare valve lifter cable for my 1958 Panther motorbike. This had the correct nipple already soldered on one end, and fitted straight into the cold start knob. A short extra length of outer cable completed the job.

The final task involved a bit of 3 dimensional thought – the overdrive micro switches. Remove the cam from the end of the shaft, turn it round and then rotate it through 90°. Then swap over the pairs of wires in the switches, adjust them as outlined in the manual and away you go.

First impressions are of a smoother tickover, less intake noise, and an engine that pulls much more smoothly at low revs.

A run down to the National revealed no problems, and a steady 60 - 70 mph cruise along mixed roads and two city centres showed a consumption approaching 35 mpg. In fact I only stopped at a garage once on the 350 miles and I wasn't sure whether to put more petrol in or to drain some out.

Should anyone out there want to try this and needs further details please contact me. I can do the mod to the carb shaft, free of charge if required.

Oh, and no she doesn't flood any more.

Steve Shone

July 1995

DUKE OF HAZARD

Whilst continuing the overhaul of my P4 '100' over the winter months, I came across two spare insulated bullet socket connectors attached to two leads emanating from the main cable harness, inside the instruments compartment.

What use could they be, they obviously had been fitted for a purpose.

This interested me and I traced them to the 2 - LH and 2 - RH winker lamps.

I like to think that the Rover engineers, with characteristic foresight, had way back in time thought about Hazard Warning Lights, and so had the harnesses manufactured with these unused bullet connector sockets added in anticipation of such future use.

With Rover having done the difficult part of the wiring, it would be easy to fit a Hazard Warning Light System, controlled from a Single Pole switch:-

'Up' for Normal Winker operation, 'Down' for Hazard operation.

The essential requirements are that:

1. The original wiring is not disturbed in any way except for the insertion of the single pole, Hazard Warning On/Off switch, which is tucked away out of sight under the dash, and connections to the Winkers made via the aforementioned bullet connectors.

2. The Hazard Warning Lights must be able to be switched ON with the car electrics in any operational position, i.e. with the ignition switched off etc.

3. The main wiring must be safe (this has already been done by the Rover Co.).

4. The Hazard Circuit must be completely isolated from the Normal Winker operation Circuit.

5. The Default condition, from any untoward situation, must always be an immediate return to Normal Winker working by returning the Hazard switch to the UP (off) position.

These conditions are achieved by using the following components.

1 - Single pole switch.

1 - Hazard Flasher Unit type. 9 FL12V with holder.

1 - 12 volt D.C. 3PDT (3 pole double throw) relay.

1 - P600A Diode.

1 - 12 volt lamp (red) with holder.

Cost approx. £10 to £12 from Maplin Electronics.

I found the ideal position for the Red Hazard Warning Indicator lamp, was to fit it out of sight, just above the instrument panel cluster. When ON the light from the lamp reflects strongly from the chrome rims of the instruments which is quite sufficient to show that the Hazard Warning Switch is ON.

Don't forget to disconnect the battery under the rear seat when working behind the instrument panel, or better still, consider fitting a battery isolator switch to the bulkhead near the starter relay, which is an ideal place, just waiting for such a switch.

I wonder if all P4 cars have a cable harness with the two spare winker bullet sockets fitted, like the harness fitted to my P4 '100'.

If not, one can always locate the winker leads source from the main junction box on the bulkhead near the steering column.

If you think that my experience will be of interest or help to anyone, I will be pleased to give you a short article with fitting instructions, together with a simple circuit diagram.

Richard Anderson   *July 1995*

SPOT THE DIFFERENCE

Yes, a British Jaeger with a sweep secondhand. How is this, you may ask!! Well we all know the problems with these little devils, stopping now and then for no apparent reason. Give them a kickstart and away they go till the next time. What with losing in the summer and gaining in the winter. This incidentally is due to the viscosity of the oil, (lubricating the mechanism) varying and causing the balance wheel to either long or short stroke. Over the years I have cleaned movements, repaired balance wheels with contact pins, replaced strikers and coils.

Well just by chance one day I was browsing in one of these cheapy arcade shops and I came across some all polastic quartz travel alarm clocks for £2.49 each. Having checked the accuracy of the movement I then stripped out the quartz mechanism to see if it could be accommodated in the case of the Jaeger, and yes with a few modifications it would.

So with a junior hacksaw, file, soldering iron, solder and wire I removed all electrical and mechanical components associated with the alarm mechanism. I then cut the circuit board away to fit into the Jaeger case. Where I had to cut away the copper track, this was hard wired back.

Next was to mount the quartz movement and backface (the part with British Jaeger printed on it) to the correct hands to back face relationship as in the Jaeger.

This was achieved by marking off the back onto 1mm thick insulation board, drilling the centre hole and then piercing the 3 face fixing holes just large enough for the original screws to cut their own threads.

Next was to drill four holes in the insulation board, two for two long 4ba screws, to fix the quartz movement to and finally assemble the whole thing in the Jaeger case, one for a small screw to accept the original hand set/start button and one for the fast/slow segmented wheel indicator. Next is to cut away as much of the insulation board as possible, but leaving a small three point mounting, this will centralise the movement and allow a light path to illuminate the front face. Next is to drill the circuit board and assemble the backface and quartz movement. The hands are the original and unless you are lucky, will need to be either opened up or soldered up and redrilled. The centre sweep has the original, though modified, black button fixed to it. Should you not require this facility thus giving more originality, cut off the sweephand and just the black button will rotate virtually unnoticeable.

The back of the Jaeger case can now be drilled to accept the 4ba screws and a hole for the hand set adjustment, Now solder neg and pos wires to the circuit board for the 1.5v AA size battery. Now blank off all holes not required to stop light escapement, and assemble and place in the Jaeger case. *Note* **The 4ba fixing screws** must pass through **grommeted holes** as should the **battery wires** and be very careful when assembling that none of the quartz movement can short out to the Jaeger case, as this will be at a 12v potential with the lamp illuminating the clock. Now make a small clip to hold the battery to the back of the clock, this and the battery **must be insulated** from the case. Now you have as near original looking British Jaeger clock that keeps good time with a bonus of telling you the time when the battery is disconnected. Not bad for £2.49 plus a week of evening work. Better and more interesting that the telly!!

P.S.

Some of you may have the later pattern back face with an extended 45° bezel, either cut it away or be very careful that nothing shorts between case and quartz movement. "Best of Luck".

Mike Coleman   *January 1996*

P4 CYLINDER HEADS

The top-end overhaul of the P4 is well documented and even the workshop manual is quite useful if followed carefully. However, there are a few failings that are not covered in the manual and it is these that I would like to highlight in the hope that they will be of use when the head is removed for inspection.

The cylinder head is quite straightforward to remove but generally speaking, the only likely snag is the removal of the temperature transmitter from the outside of the head (not '95', '110'). The brass face of the bulb has usually been overtightened to the taper seat in the head and being dissimilar metals corrode together. They should be assembled with vaseline or copperslip on the seat and threads but rarely are. The capillary tube attached to the bulb is very delicate and care must be taken not to bend it as this will surely fracture it and it will become useless. If this does happen the whole unit from dial to bulb will have to be replaced.

Care must also be taken with the oil-feed pipe into the rear of the head. It should be undone using a well fitting ring spanner and try not to bend the pipe in any way, otherwise it will be difficult to restart the thread on re-assembly. Always drain the block as well as the radiator before commencing work, otherwise you will find some of the cylinders full of coolant on removal.

Once removed, the head should first be inspected for excessive corrosion in the water-ways. By laying the old cylinder head gasket on top of the face you will be able to see how far any corrosion has eroded beyond the cut-outs of the gasket. For example, if it has travelled too close to the combustion chamber, a bolt hole or too near the edge of the head. If the corrosion is excessive the easiest way out is to try and locate a head that is in better condition. These secondhand heads are not usually too expensive to buy, but the problem of course, is finding one. The other option is to find an engineering firm that is able and willing to machine out the corroded pockets and then fill with aluminium weld. This is a highly specialised job and could well be very expensive, but once welded the water-ways can be machined out and the head re-faced.

Refacing must be carried out correctly, otherwise it is better not to machine it at all. Most engineering firms will fly-cut the head on a milling machine. This is not good practice as the surface finish is not fine enough. Rover always specified that the heads were ground on a surface grinder (not plough-grinder) and then polished in a straight line using 1000 wet-or-dry paper adhered to a flat plate at least the width of the head and lubricated with paraffin. The heads should not be clamped down for machining but should be bolted to two flat plates (steel) about 4½" x 6" x ¾" using ⁵⁄₁₆" bolts through two of the valve guides. The plates should have a ⁵⁄₁₆" tapped hole in the centre of them for the bolts to screw into. These plates will then hold on to the magnetic chuck of the surface grinder. ('110' heads will require a shallow counter-bore in the plates for the protruding guide to sit into)

Nine out of ten heads I refurbish are warped to some degree. At best they will need .005" removed to clean them, but I have known them to need .010". Incidentally, on the '110' head the step-down to the boss for the waterpump to meet the O seal should measure .125" (3.175mm). If too much is removed from the cylinder head face, the gap could become too small and over compress the seal.

Invariably the by-pass holes in the head between the pistons are clogged up. These must be carefully drilled out, using a hand-drill with ¾₆" drill bit. The position of these can be ascertained by using the gasket as a template.

When stripping the head prior to machining, always number the rockers before removal. Once removed, the rocker pads should be examined for any indentations of the valve stem, and for accurate tappet settings should be stoned smooth by pressing down on an oiled oil-stone in a to-and-fro action following the radius of the face.

Take note also of the rocker spacers (not '110' or '80') these can wear to such an extent that the rocker face is not central with the valve stem and can lead to noisy inlet valve clatter. They are not expensive and are well worth replacing.

Check that the by-pass hole at the base of the thermostat aperture is clear, if not, drill out using a hand-drill and a ¼" drill bit. This is not easy to check on the '110' as it is drilled at an angle, an air-line is useful here.

Of course, before any machining is undertaken it is an ideal opportunity to have the head professionally cleaned. Try to avoid grit or bead blasting because this can leave nasty abrasives hidden in the many crevices of the complex casting. The best method of cleaning is vapour-blasting which does not leave any residue and gives a good satin finish.

While the head is off, clean the spark plug threads, ideally with a 14mm tap or an old plug with 3 or 4 slots cut longitudinally into the thread.

Before fitting the head, make sure that the threads in the engine block are thoroughly clean and free of any oil that may be lurking down the bottom of the holes. If this is not done the cylinder head bolt could force any trapped oil to crack the block, because oil cannot be compressed.

When the head is built and prior to fitting, smear its face with an even coating of clean engine oil, also the engine block. Do not use grease, hylomar or hermetite. Torque the head down in increments of 10 ft lbs until the required torque is met. Always use a good quality torque-wrench and never guess!

Never use a wax-stat type thermostat, it must be of the bellows type and use a strong solution of antifreeze on re-filling and do not forget to bleed the system when the engine is at full temperature.

Stan Johnstone

January 1997

AVON TYRES RECOMMENDATIONS FOR TYRE STORAGE

Introduction
In view of the harmful influence of temperature, humidity and light, inside storage is essential.

Humidity
The store room should be cool, dry and moderately ventilated. Moist conditions should be avoided. Care must be taken to ensure no condensation occurs.

Tyres destined for retreading/repairing must be thoroughly dried out beforehand.

Light
There should be protection from sunlight and strong artificial light with a high ultra-violet content. Room lighting with ordinary incandescent lamps is preferable to fluorescent tubes.

Temperature
The storage temperature should be below 25°C and preferably below 15°C. At temperatures exceeding 25°C certain forms of deterioration may be accelerated sufficiently to affect the ultimate service life. Direct contact with pipes and radiators must be avoided.

The effects of low temperature are not permanently deleterious, but can cause the products to stiffen. Care should be taken therefore to avoid distorting them during handling at that temperature. When they are taken from low temperature storage for immediate use, their temperature should be raised to approximately 20°C throughout before they are put into service.

Oxygen

As ozone is particularly harmful, storage rooms should not contain any equipment generating ozone such as fluorescent lighting, mercury vapour lamps, electric motors or other electrical discharges. Combustion gases and vapours which may produce ozone via photochemical processes should also be excluded.

Solvents, fuels, lubricants, chemicals, acids, disinfectants and the like should not be kept in the store rooms. Rubber solutions should be stored in a separate room and the administrative regulations on the storage and handling of inflammable liquids must be observed.

Deformation

Products should be stored in a relaxed condition free from tension, compression or other deformation since these may cause cracking or permanent distortion.

Rotation of stock

To avoid deterioration storage time must be minimised. Stocks should be issued from the stores in rotation so that those remaining in storage are of the latest manufacture or delivery.

Short term storage

For short term storage (up to 4 weeks) tyres can be stacked horizontally, one on top of another, on wooden gratings but the height of the stacks should not exceed 1.20 metres. After 4 weeks the tyres should be restacked, reversing the order of the tyres.

Long term storage.

For long term storage tyres should be stored upright in a single layer on shelf racks with at least 10cm clearance above the floor. To avoid deformation it is advisable to rotate them slightly once a month.

Tubes

Tyre tubes should either be slightly inflated, dusted with talcum and placed in the tyres, or stored in a deflated condition in small stacks – maximum height 50cm – in the compartments of shelf racks with a level bottom. Slatted pallettes are not suitable since they might apply pressure at particular points.

If tubes are supplied by the manufacturers in cartons or wrapped in film, they should be left in these because the packing provides some degree of protection against contamination, oxygen and the effect of light.

Flaps
Flaps should preferably be placed with the tubes, inside tyres, but if stored separately they should be laid flat on shelves free from contamination from dust, grease and moisture. Never suspend them – this can cause deformation and elongation.

For further information please contact: Avon Tyres Ltd., Melksham, Wiltshire SN12 8AA. Telephone 01225 703101. Telex: 44142. Fax: 01225 707880.

ROVER P4 SCUTTLE AND A-POST REPAIR TECHNIQUES

Barry Kensett of Yorkshire has produced this excellent practical article on welding on the P4, including the difficult A-post area.

In the late fifties and sixties, the corrosion resistance designed and built into our cars was far inferior to current day practice. The Rover may be considered to be better built than most but some of the design features are appalling to today's standards. The materials and techniques available were also inferior in most respects, it was unusual to use zinc coated materials (unless you had a Volvo) which were difficult to spot weld and paint and were more costly than bright steel. There were no effective interlay compounds which could be spot-welded through to give protection in the many flange joints, there were many closed boxes in the body structure which had no internal paint or wax treatments and little thought was given to drainage leading to water traps.

The area behind the front wheels of the P4 is very prone to corrosion and it is extremely rare to find a car that has not been damaged in this area. Figure 1 illustrates the components likely to be affected to some degree.

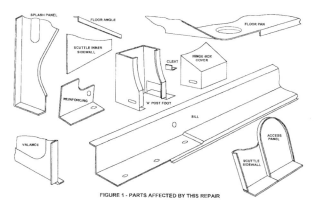

FIGURE 1 - PARTS AFFECTED BY THIS REPAIR

Figure 1. Parts affected by this repair.

It is not difficult to review the phases of the corrosion process which starts with the effective blasting of the splash panel and valance behind the front wheels with sand, water and saline solution. The rubber flap seal on the splash panel may not be a good seal. Once the splash panel is penetrated, the saline solution is partially trapped in the closed box which did not originally have the benefit of any drain holes. The bottom of the sill extension, the scuttle sidewall and access panel (this exists to let the spot-welder arm in manufacture) and the parts around the base of the A-post are immersed and quickly corrode, particularly where the many flanged and spot welded joints provide electrolytic batteries. Keeping the car in a nice warm garage would accelerate the process! Rain from the top adds to the problem as the only escape path for water draining from the windscreen and bonnet area is down the outside of the scuttle and onto the A-post from above. It is possible to see into the base of the A-post through the access hole behind the scuttle trim panel but this only reveals part of the problem area.

Meanwhile a second attack would be taking place once the inner valance is penetrated allowing water into the trap formed by the horizontal spot-welded joint between the scuttle inner sidewall and the vertical face of the sill extension. A path is now open for the sand-blasting to strike the floor in the footwell area around the handbrake apertures and perforation here usually occurs. Once the box around the lower door hinge is perforated, water enters this area affecting the door hinge itself and then running back under the sill mats to perforate the sill from above. Eventually the sill structure around the body mount starts to break out compounded by the breakdown of the outer end of the front outrigger which is another repair topic in its own right.

There is no standard repair for the areas of damage, the rate of corrosion depends on the usage of the car. It will be different on both sides of the car and the course of events will be modified by any superficial repairs which may have been carried out during the car's life.

On my own car I knew that the usual problems existed but were masked by a plate which had been welded to the bottom of the front wing and folded up and tacked to the scuttle sidewall. This was obviously done some years ago as it had perforated in a couple of places. On the other side it was possible to hear the rust debris bouncing around if the bottom was tapped with a hand! The timing of the repair was eventually precipitated by the breakdown of the body mounting in the sill and the outrigger and I decided to tackle the whole area as a winter project.

The Repair Process

It is necessary to remove the front wings as described in the workshop manual; in my case it was necessary to cut the wing at the base due to the temporary repair. The front valance had also been tack welded to the wing! The wing must come off before the doors to get access to the bolt through the A-post; the hinge bolt through the sill will probably need grinding off. The doors and hinges can then be removed and care must be taken with the sponge seals unless they are due for replacement. I would recommend that the bonnet is also removed. Front seats, carpets and handbrake will need to come out if the floor is perforated and the aluminium trim strip along the top of the sill will need removal followed by any insulation pads within welding range. The front screws of this trim may need the gentle application of an impact driver to loosen them. Underseal will need to be removed in areas where welding is needed; a hot air gun and scraper is the easiest way to do this. The rubber seal on the splash panel should be removed if it hasn't dropped off.

Offside 1 – Before

The car must be raised and if a lift or pit is not available, I find that lifting the car about two feet is about the right compromise between access and arm reach. I removed the front outriggers as these were also due for replacement and access to the sill is easier without these.

Some repair parts are available, I found that the sill extension section and the scuttle side access panel save some manufacturing time. The section available for the scuttle sidewall was a quarter of an inch too narrow for my car; I made a piece to fit. I used 18 swg mild steel sheet for all repairs and I made patterns with card first before cutting the metal. I use a nibbler to roughly shape the sheet and Gilbows and file to finish off. All folding for this job can be carried out in the vice with a few bars and a hard wood block. Before attacking with a saw and grinder, the job can do with a lot of hard looking at to determine the best place for joining to sound metal. The old joiner's adage "keep your wood as long as you can as long as you can" applies. Care must be taken in not cutting away too much at one go and risk losing the shape.

Offside 2 – Before

The scuttle sidewall should be cut back to sound metal and the access panel ground out to help access to the sidewall.

The sill repair section is sized to lap over rather than butt weld to the sill; this means that any sound sill can be left in place which assists with alignment. If there is damage to the sill behind the coverage of the repair piece this should be repaired with inserts, butt welded in place. Due to the corrosion trap at the top flange of the front end of the sill, it is unlikely that there is sufficient material hanging from the scuttle inner wall to meet the new section. This must either be replaced by a lap welded extension or plug welded to the angle on the floor although the latter is tricky due to the thickness of metal on the down hanging flange and the difficult access. The sill repair can be clamped in place at the body mount position and lined up with the remains of the splash panel. When confident on position, the holes for the body mount hinge bolt can be drilled to allow the section to be bolted up.

An A-post foot can then be repaired as necessary; on one side I had to replace the front wall, back and base. The hinge box cover can then be welded around the outside and the hinge should be offered up at this stage to make sure that there is adequate clearance.

The floor pan should be repaired before the sill is welded in for better access. I used insert repairs but lap welds would be satisfactory here if you do not mind the appearance. Shaping the pressed area around the handbrake hole is a bit tricky; I beat it roughly to shape on the bench, welded it in and then heated the double curvature to bright red and tapped into shape in situ.

The sill extension can then be attached permanently and for this I found that bronze welding is best as it penetrates the lap better than welding. This is attached at the rear end of the horizontal and vertical laps from below the car and to the A-post foot faces from the top. The scuttle inner wall is then connected to the vertical flange and I used rivets here to enable the use of a chromate interlay material to prevent corrosion at this vulnerable joint. Plug welding would be satisfactory and as good as the original build.

The scuttle access panel can now be offered up and the forward section of sidewall made to suit. This is butt welded to the sidewall and the access panel is edge welded in place. The aft flange is heated and tapped back close to the A-post and welded. The bottom flanges are bronze welded to the sill section (remove the zinc coating first).

The splash panel can now be cut back to sound metal and a new section fabricated and butt welded in place. Similarly the valance needs an insert repair and finally the four flanges of the valance, sill, sidewall and splash panel are edge welded. I sealed all joints in this area with bronze weld to help weather resistance and close up holes exposed to the front wheels.

If the splash panel is badly corroded higher up, it is possible to obtain a new repair panel. Mine was not bad enough for this but was perforated intermittently adjacent to the forward projecting flange. Welding in this area would not be successful, there is insufficient sound metal to go at and the heat would set fire to the trim behind the dash. I straightened and ground the flange to the original projection. I then made a section of angle to fit onto the face of the splash panel far enough away to be lap welded and flanged up and over the projecting flange and clamped with chromate interlay rather like a Mini body seam.

All metal was then primed with a damp resistant primer (e.g. Rustoleum 769), seams sealed with 3M body caulk, black enamelled and waxoyl black underseal to finish.

Bottom door hinges should be checked for wear and repaired if necessary (see Overdrive No. 95, March 1994, Page 20) before replacing doors. Front wings and bonnet are replaced as described in workshop manual. With care to rustproofing, the above repair job should never need to be done again.

Offside 1 – After

Offside 2 – After

Floor pan repair

ROVER P4 FRONT OUTRIGGER REPLACEMENT

The front outriggers on the Rover chassis are subjected to the blast of water and salt from the front wheels and not surprisingly are a common corrosion point. The forward face and the bottom section usually suffer first and these can be patched. When the outer face which supports the body mounting starts to break up there is little access to do a permanent repair and a more drastic treatment is required. An additional major problem is caused by the collection of water in the bottom of the outrigger which cannot escape but can penetrate the joint with the main chassis member and corrode through the chassis at this point.

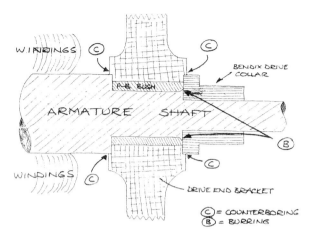

CROSS-SECTION OF DRIVE END BRACKET (NOT TO SCALE)

This diagram first appeared in Freewheel, the bulletin of the R.S.R.

The best access to carry out replacement is with the body off; I have heard of people who raise the body about a foot which can usually be done in the garage with normal lifting tackle. I have also heard of people waving their welding torch blind in the gap between the outrigger and the floor – the mind boggles!

Access in floor to remove and replace top flange and outrigger.

Faced with the breakout of the body mounting I talked to a few experts and decided to change the outriggers without removing the body, and to get access to the top I cut two access holes in the floor nine inches by three inches using a nobble (had I used a grinder there was a danger of nicking the hydraulic pipes on the offside). I then jacked the car up about two feet and removed the master cylinder and its rod along with the handbrake and its front rod. It is then possible to cut the outriggers off with an angle grinder and clean up the faces to receive replacements. There is a slight complication on the offside with the master cylinder mounting bracket; I cut this by gouging into the outrigger to leave the bracket intact for welding to the new outrigger. I needn't have bothered as the new outrigger sat in a slightly different position and the bracket had to be extended anyway. There is no need to take the bracket off of the chassis member.

Rearside outrigger.

Once the outriggers were off I found that the chassis was rusted through where water had collected in the bottom flange but this damage had not extended beyond the outrigger flange. I therefore was able to weld an insert into the chassis before fitting the new outriggers.

I elected to use the ready made new outriggers which are on the market and which fitted reasonably well. The flanges were long but were easily cut back. The height was about an eighth of an inch too small to fit over my chassis but I cut the weld for about one inch on the bottom flange which enabled it to be sprung open sufficiently. The cut was then welded up. I had to trim the vertical faces very slightly to get a close fit.

The outer end of the outrigger was located in the sill using new mountings but I used a bolt with a turned down shank to set the outrigger 0.1" high to ensure that it carried its share of body weight. The zinc plate was removed from all welding faces.

Whilst I usually prefer gas welding, I used MIG to attach the outrigger to the chassis as the amount of heat needed would have set fire to the underseal on the floor. The welding is very straightforward but needs at least 130 amps to get the right penetration (this is about the limit on a 13 amp plug). Bronze welding would be strong enough and use less heat but I felt that the slight pitting on the chassis would make it difficult to tin properly, particularly on the overhead weld where balls of molten metal up the sleeve are a hazard at the best of times. I should have painted the inside of the outriggers before welding them on; it would have been a lot easier on the bench!

As mentioned earlier, I extended the master cylinder bracket to meet the outrigger face which sat a little forward of the original. I lapped the extension onto the old bracket and fillet welded it to the outrigger being careful to leave space for the jacking point.

The undersize bolt was removed from the body mounting by removing the bolts through the outrigger that provide clearance to extract it. The sill was then jacked to line up the bolt hole and a packer was made to fill the gap between the mount and the sill. The jacking points, handbrake, master cylinder and rods were then replaced. I finally made up a pair of panels to close up the floor.

Rearside outrigger.

Barry Kensett

WATER ON P4 SPARK PLUGS

I was interested to read Michael Walkling's letter in the September issue of Overdrive as my '110' occasionally suffered from the same problem – wet spark plugs as a result of water dripping through the clips holding down the central chrome strip on top of the bonnet. I can recommend the following solution.

Expanded foam pipe lagging comes in 1 metre lengths and is pre-slit so that it can be clipped around pipes. There is a large flange running under the centre line of the bonnet through which the chrome strip clips pass and hence the water. The pipe lagging can be pushed onto this flange. Any water that enters will run down the central hole of the pipe lagging and will drain down by the radiator. Because it is so light it does not require any glue or other fixing, and it actually looks quite neat. It takes about 30 seconds to fit so those who are worried about corrosion due to lack of air circulation or the possibility of it coming off on a long journey can remove it and re fit it when the car is going to be parked in wet conditions. The foam is heat resistant and flame retardant, so even if it does come off no real damage should result. You will need just under a metre, and the lagging for 15mm pipes which has a total diameter of about 40mm is ideal. My local DIY store sells a pack of 5 x 1 metre lengths for £2.50. I fitted this to my car in October and have had no problems since.

Hugh Richards   *March 1998*

FRONT SUSPENSION OVERHAUL –

Alternative Methods and Renovation Tips

"Eight inches from yer balls, is that all you've got?" exclaimed the missus! I looked up from the November issue of Overdrive, gobsmacked, only to notice that she had been reading the notes I had made of the project I was to undertake during the Christmas break.

Yes eight inches ground clearance from the underside of the radius arm balls, this relates to the workshop manuals normal ride height into which you are expected to tighten up all the relevant nuts and bolts after the overhaul of any part of the suspension. Unfortunately my garage is not blessed with a pit, and even if it were, where on earth does one obtain those special half moon wheels to gain access to the top link pin nuts? Perhaps Stan-Stan the Rover Man may have a set tucked away!!

It was with this in mind, and the fact that a good many of us P4 owners are akinned to our beloved vehicles, i.e. - past our prime, have difficulty negotiating within confined spaces, round and cuddly and built for **comfort** not **speed**. So to this end the following technique was devised:

1.   Check that the tyre pressures are correct.
2.   Give the vehicle a settling bounce.
3.   Measure and **note** the distances between the tops of the front wheel arches and their respective hub centres.
4.   Place a spirit level across the front overriders or numberplate box and apply a piece of tape either side of the bubble. And if you have a memory like mine, a piece of tape one side of the level and on its adjacent overrider, so it goes back the right way round, saves a lot of frustration later on.

You can now raise the whole front of the vehicle to give a comfortable working height at the rear of the radius arms. I prefer to have three wheels at a time supporting the vehicle, using wooden blocks under the wheel of the opposite side to which I am working, and supporting the working side at the front chassis end.

Level off the vehicle to the marked spirit level and don't forget to take as many safety precautions as possible in stabilizing the vehicle, **remember you will be underneath it**!!

I usually chock the rear wheels, have a support in close proximity about $\frac{1}{16}$" at the junction of the front outrigger - main chassis - gearbox crossmember and not relying solely on the handbrake, wind in the master cylinders to foot pedal connecting rod tight, this gives three wheels locked hydraulically.

'Over the top' you may say, but I live to write this article!!

Now for the removal of the springs. Forget the trolley jack, chain and Rover Part No. 262774. Obtain from your local DIY Store 4 lengths of $\frac{5}{16}$" whit or M8 studding (these are usually supplied in 12" lengths) 8 full nuts, 4 half nuts and 4 washers.

Disconnect the torsion bar and shock absorber from the spring support plate. Loosen all 10 bolts fixing the bottom link arms to the spring support plate, just enough to slide in the half nuts. Now remove one of the two bolts closest to the centre of the vehicle. Spin a full nut followed by a washer about 1" down a piece of studding, insert a half nut in the gap and screw up the studding so as it projects enough to accept a full nut on top and tighten up. Now spin bottom full nut and washer up finger tight to support plate. Repeat this operation for the fourth bolt along and then both operations for the other side of the support plate. You will note that the four studding are directly below the bolts for the top tie straps. Remove remaining six bolts and you are now ready to wind down the spring. Apply some oil to the studs to help things along and wind down the nuts evenly. To speed things up a little, I used a box spanner like that in the Rover tool tray and a short series ring spanner on the other end, so as it rotates between the studdings.

Although this is not a fast method, about ten minutes, it does in my opinion give a degree of safety to the DIY mechanic. Now dismantle the rest of the bottom link assembly.

Thoroughly inspect all components for corrosion, the support plates are prone to this and also the coned bump stop both rot badly as there is no drain facility. Support plates should be replaced, bump stops can be reclaimed by prefabricating a new cone and welding on. I had to do one of mine.

Check the bush housings for corrosion as any amount will drastically reduce the life of the new bushes. These should be polished smooth with emery cloth. A piece of ⅜" dia. rod with a slot cut up it, to take the emery cloth, and fitted in an electric or battery drill works well or an engineers bearing scraper and emery cloth to finish.

Before fitting back together, the cone bump stop should have two ⁵⁄₁₆" holes drilled at 180° as close to the bottom as possible and aligned front to back on assembly. The spring support plate should also be drilled with a ⁵⁄₁₆" drain hole at its lowest point, that is facing out towards the wheel. Reassembly of the bottom link arms can now take place. Use a liberal coating of red rubber grease on the bushes, pins and housings. Leave all four nuts loose by a couple of turns on the link pins. *Note: do not fit spring, bump stop and support plate at this stage.*

Now for the radius arm ball. With a jack about twelve inches away from the radius arm housing, firmly support, but not enough so as to lift the vehicle, the opposite sides radius arm. Remove the five bolts and lower the bottom half of the housing. Lower radius arm and ball, clean up as required, replace ball with red rubber grease, bottom half of housing using only the four vertical bolts and leave them loose by a couple of turns.

The top link arm is next. Before dismantling, tie back the top anchor bush housing to the shock absorber mounting bracket to take any strain off the brake hose. Clean bush housings as previously mentioned. Now underneath the inboard bush housing attached to the chassis, you will find a hole about ¾" dia. in the chassis, also one about ⅜" dia. when viewed from the engine compartment. These are the points of ingress that fills up the bump stops, they will need to be sealed off.

Now re-assemble with red rubber grease leaving the nuts on the pins loose as before. *Note: do not fit the top link bump stop at this stage.*

Now raise the hub assembly to the previously measured distance between wheel arch and hub centre, and pack in position between the top link arm and the rebound plate on the chassis. This is your **ride height.** You can now tighten **all** nuts and bolts with ease. Remove the jack from under the radius arm. If you are going to do the opposite side of the vehicle without driving the car, there is no need at this stage to fit the horizontal bolt on the radius arm housing.

The cone bump stop, shims, spring and support plate assembly are next. After waxoyling everything, including up inside the chassis, fit and lock up the studdings as before and wind up the spring, fitting the six bolts before removing the studdings and replacing with the final four bolts. Last but not least, jack up suspension to remove packing and fit top link bump stop. Repeat for the opposite side of the vehicle.

I hope this has been informative and interesting and should anyone else have some additional ideas or improvements, let Overdrive know so as we can all benefit.

Best of luck

Mike Coleman (Mr. Modification)   *March 1998*

SAFETY BELTS

I share Steve Shone's concern for safety as detailed in his article of January 1998. We quickly fitted front seat belts after buying our '105S' eleven years ago and have fitted a variety of rear seat belts with the birth and growing up of our three daughters.

The youngest has always sat in the middle of the rear seat where the child's seat fits conveniently high on the centre arm rest. This has been a popular position as it gives a good view of the road between the occupants of the front seats (i.e. mum and dad!). In this position the two lower belts pass between the seat cushion and squab and are anchored near the transmission tunnel. The two upper straps have been secured by drilling through the parcel shelf into the two brackets beneath (I would welcome advice as to whether these are really up to the job). As the children have grown older I have had to devise increasingly complicated arrangements of angle iron to spread the load and provide fittings for three separate belts. I was never completely satisfied with these arrangements and wondered how well they would have coped in a serious accident.

I was pleased to discover when attending the Guild spares day in 1995 (I think) that Phil Beton had three sets of original Rover Co. rear seat belts which I snapped up right away. I bet not many members know that Rover listed seat belts when the P4 was in production. They are listed as Part No. 316921 made by Irvin. I was very fortunate to obtain these as Phil subsequently had numerous enquiries in response to an advert which he had earlier placed in Overdrive. Whilst it is marvellous to have the original belts, even more useful are the fittings and fitting instructions which came with them. The two lower anchor points are in the inner wing and near the transmission tunnel in roughly the same positions as described by Steve Shone in his letter. These are located with 'U' bolts and re-inforced steel plates.

A purpose made bracket is supplied for the upper anchor point (for the shoulder strap). These are 'handed' so each kit has two, thereby allowing fitting of the belt on either side of the back seat. These brackets attach to the boot hinge support using the existing bolts, thus no drilling (or angle iron!) is needed at this point. A small modification is made by cutting a slot at the front of the parcel shelf allowing the shoulder strap to pass neatly through and over the back of the seat. This bracket seems to me to be the key to safe and neat fitting of rear seat belts and should provide an anchor point for any three point static belt.

I have had a word with Peter Rabjohn who is willing to look into reproduction of these brackets by the Guild if there is sufficient demand. We have agreed that members should in the first instance contact me if they are interested.

I am able to provide photocopies of the fitting instructions (Part No. 316922) for rear seat belts and likewise (Part No. 316935) for front seat belts. Incidentally Rover also supplied a special plate to provide anchorage for the shoulder straps of the front seat belt on the B/C post. This neatly fits behind the trim panel.

If you would like the fitting instructions for the front or rear belts please send a large stamped addressed envelope (each set is four pages) plus one first class stamp (two if you want front and rear) to cover the cost of photocopying, to myself at 10 Elfort Road, London, N5 1AZ. Do let me know if you are interested in the brackets for the rear belts so that if there is sufficient demand I can ask Peter to look into reproducing them for the club.

As well as contributing to the safety of the rear seat passengers in the event of an accident, seat belts also locate the children in one place and give them the message that travelling by car (whilst being great fun and particularly rewarding in a P4) is also a serious business. Having developed a great interest in the literature of the 50's and 60's when I was editing the Year Book, I was interested to see that one of the strongest arguments against the use of seat belts was that children would not be able to keep still and would not put up with being confined. We have not found this a problem with our daughters, perhaps because we started when they were too young to know any difference.

Best wishes and safe driving.

Bob McGavin

March 1998

IMPROVING AUNTIE'S REAR END

    Here is my modification to the boot hinge mechanism which instead of relying on the inner wheel arch as a mounting, now uses the boot floor as it's anchor point. Some years ago I replaced the rear inner arches of my P4. I couldn't bear the thought of introducing seven bolt holes into perfectly watertight arches and so was born the idea for this modification.

Have two L-shaped brackets made up out of ⅛" mild steel plate – 2" base, 5" in height and 12" in length. Now trim back one end of each bracket to allow for the rearward rake of the rear seat bulkhead. With the bracket pushed snugly up against the wheel arch, drill three holes through the boot floor at points 1", 5" and 8" from the rearmost end of the brackets. It will be noted at this stage that the brackets will cross over a boot rib pressing. Two spacers of ¼" mild steel needs to be placed either side of the rib, under the bracket. Under the boot floor will be needed a plate of mild steel with three nuts welded to its underside lining up with the three bolts coming down from the boot.

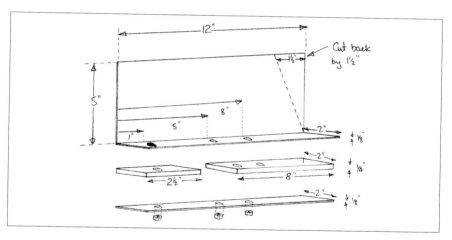

Now before marking out the remaining bolt holes please take out the hinge and trunnion bar and make sure that the pin on one and the hole in the other are serviceable. the pins on both of my hinges were almost "sawn" through! So having rectified any problems here, relocate the hinge and then mark out the four holes that will secure the vertical "leg" to the new bracket. It will now be necessary to take out the new bracket in order to correctly position the trunnion bracket.

Position the trunnion bracket so that it is resting on the foot of the new bracket. Mark and drill out the lowermost hole at a distance of 7⅛" from the nearest of the first group of holes previously drilled. Now tilt the trunnion bracket to an angle of 77° from the horizontal, mark and drill out the remaining two upper holes.

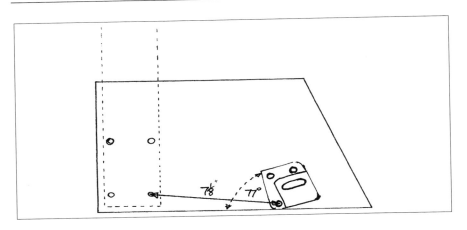

Bolt the assembly together applying plenty of grease to all moving parts, re-tension the compression springs and there you have it. The boot lid will now leap open to its maximum height and stay there. the stresses have been taken out of and away from the wheel arches and the whole thing will remain completely concealed by the original boot trim. Yes it will all fit snugly behind. Throw away that broom handle!

Any member wishing to evaluate the modification please give me a ring 0151 334 3858 and you will be more than welcome to come around and examine first hand.

Keith Hunter   *July 1998*

CORROSION IN BRAKE BLEEDERS

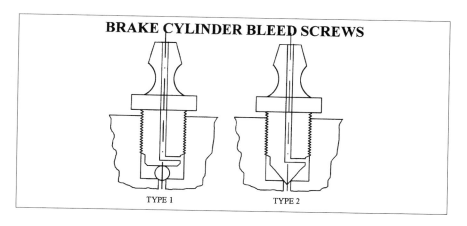

When I last carried out some work on the P4, I had broken down the brake system and it was necessary to bleed the hydraulics. I pressurised the reservoir to blow my system through and the air came out easily enough although it is a job I hate; the fluid is really the most unpleasant of substances.

I sustained pressure on the pedal for a while to check that there were no leaks and then went for a road test. After a few miles the brake fluid level light came on; my first thought was that the micro switch on the hand brake was set a little fine, but on checking, the lever did not put it out, and so I stopped to inspect. I had lost most of the container of fluid which was now around the back plate of the rear offside wheel.

The problem eventually turned out to be corrosion of the little ball bearing under the bleeder screw, which having been disturbed when the brakes were bled, had seated across the corrosion and was not sealing. I replaced the balls, and all is well. I hate to think where I would have ended up if I did not have the system with a fluid level warning.

There are two types of bleeder fitted to P4's and these are illustrated in the drawings here. It is possible to fit the conical screws in place of the ball and plain screw type, but the ball must be removed - your magnetised screwdriver will get it out. I stayed with the same arrangement as original, but put new balls in; either is technically satisfactory. I suspect my failure to detect the leak on static test was because the servo was not on and probably

I did not get the pressure high enough to reveal the problem.

As an aside, another P4 owner told me that he was fed up with the bright warning light burning his eyeballs whenever he put the hand brake on and he had disconnected the warning switch. I had to point out to him that the main reason for the hand brake warning is a routine bulb test function without which you could lose fluid and not get a warning if the bulb has failed. The servicing instructions also call for a routine check on the float switch.

Barry Kensett   *July 1998*

REAR AXLE PINION OIL SEAL REPLACEMENT

I would say that at least 80% of the P4's I have been privileged to work on, have a most common complaint – oil seepage from the rear axle pinion seal. Most of them appear to have been leaking for many years, and quite often, the axle casing is at least an inch bigger than it should be! One good thing about this of course, is that it stops the casing from rusting up and at the same time keeps the rear section of the chassis in a 'gooey' but protected state. The bad side of course, is the fact that you cannot tell how much oil is left inside to lubricate those most stressed and vital parts, unless you make very regular checks.

To replace the pinion seal, which of course, is the only answer, is not a difficult job, just messy and slightly awkward if you haven't got a hoist or a pit.

The first job is to drain the oil from the unit, this could range in volume from an eggcupful to $3^1/_2$ pints. Then to make life as easy as possible, get the car jacked up prior to work. It helps to elevate the front of the car first, either on sturdy axle stands sitting under the front of the radius arms, or ideally, with railway sleeper-type blocks under the front wheels, approx 6" between tyre and ground. Whenever possible, leave the road wheels on the car, and in this particular job, this can be done, because they will not get in the way. You can then jack the rear of the car up, and support it, using axle stands under the axle casing, next to the road spring supports.

Once the car is jacked up fairly high off the ground, and you are happy that it is well supported, you can then clamber underneath and start by

152

cleaning the area around the pinion seal housing. When this is spotlessly clean, you can then start dismantling. It is most important that everything is clean before you remove the seal housing from the front of the differential, because debris could drop into the unit and thus quickly destroy the bevel pinion front bearing.

Undo the rear propshaft flange from the driving flange on the differential. Then remove the split pin just inside the driving flange and undo the nut securing the flange, handbrake fully on! This nut should be torqued to 85lb/ft but sometimes can take some shifting.

Slide off the flange and then knock back the tab locks from the six bolts around the housing, and then undo the bolts and remove the housing. Whilst you are fitting the new seal, it is wise to wrap a piece of clean rag around the diff so that dirt is kept away from the exposed bearing. Clean the housing, then tap out the old seal. Meticulously clean the recess in the housing, smear hylomar around the OD of the new seal and with the use of a vice and two flat pieces of wood, gently squeeze the seal fully into the housing with the open end facing inwards.

Making sure the mating faces are clean, smear hylomar over the face of the pinion seal housing. With a smear of vaseline on the flange, push it on to the splines of the bevel pinion, replace the washer and the nut and gently nip up the nut, this should hold the housing in its central position. Then replace the lock tabs and bolts and tighten the housing to the axle body. Make sure the prop shaft bolts are fitted in the flange and tighten the pinion nut to approx 85lb/ft aligning with a relative hole for the split pin. The propshaft can then be replaced and bolted to the flange.

The only possible snag in doing this job, is the fact that the flange diameter around which the seal runs, may on occasion, be 'grooved' with wear, right where the seal runs. Even worse, it can be pitted in this vital sealing area, and quite honestly is only fit for the knacker's yard! Not all is lost though, because if you are lucky, you may be able to get hold of a double lipped seal, which, as its name implies, seals not only in two places, but either side of the original 'track' of the single lip type. If you cannot get hold of a double lipped seal, you will have to find a donor flange, with a good surface finish for the single lipped seal.

Stan Johnstone

July 1999

P4 HANDBRAKE MECHANISM MOD

You may be interested in the attached sketch which shows a very simple modification to the P4 handbrake operating ratchet mechanism, to overcome the well known problem of the pawl tending to pull sideways as the brake is applied, and causing the pawl to sometimes "jump back" a notch, resulting in a poor handbrake hold.

The mod is not intended to mask excessive wear in the various bearings or pawl, which of course must be maintained in good order; but having applied this mod; (which consists of a steel plate of 18-20 SWG steel, with holes drilled to fit over the studs which take the usual fixing washers), I have experienced no further problems over the past year. In fact it is now a pleasure to be able to park on steep hills again with complete confidence! (The steel plate may be adjusted with packing washers if necessary such that a nice 'sliding fit', without any undue sideplay is achieved and should, of course, be maintained well greased).

C.H. Ford *1990 Yearbook*

P4 HANDBRAKE MODIFICATION

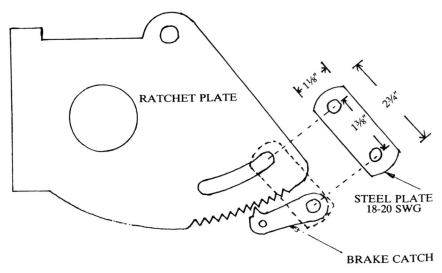

PLAN YOUR MAINTENANCE PROGRAMME

Your trusty P4 will remain so, provided you treat it with respect and carry out the necessary maintenance. It helps if you can stick to a programme so that you don't end up having to spend a week just catching up on the various jobs that need to be done. This is to say everything does not need to be done at one time. You can spread out the work to be done according to your mileage, often I think, unfortunately, governed by the insurance companies.

By way of a suggestion I would recommend the following procedure, bearing in mind your particular mileage. If for example you cover 5,000 miles per annum you will need to do two engine oil changes a year. Whereas if you only do 1,500 miles a year one oil change would suffice. That is to say, the recommended period being 3,000 miles the oil would remain in the engine for two years. This is not good because oil deteriorates even just standing, so it would therefore be safer to change the oil once a year on a 1,500 miles a year schedule.

Always change the oil when the engine is at full running temperature i.e. after approximately a 15 mile run. Obviously the filter will need to be replaced with a new canister at every oil change.

Clean the spark plugs on a yearly basis regardless of mileage (unless you are doing in excess of 10,000) and reset the gap. Change the contact breakers (points) after about 5,000 miles and if they look particularly sooty replace the condenser as well. Reset the points gap and check the ignition timing. Examine the plug leads at each end to see that no corrosion has taken place and check that the contact is clean between the suppressors and spark plug dust cover (not fitted on '95' and '110').

Tappets should be checked and readjusted if necessary at 5,000 mile intervals. These are best done with the inlets hot (about 15 mile run) and the exhaust 'overnight' cold.

The coolant should be drained and flushed every two years regardless of mileage and refilled with a strong solution of antifreeze (about 7 pints of antifreeze). At this point the thermostat (must be bellows/alcohol type) should be removed and checked in near boiling water to see that it is opening fully.

The swivel pins, steering box, and steering idler levels should be checked every 5,000. The swivel pin reservoirs are best checked using a dip stick made from ⅛" dia wire (an old wire coat hanger is ideal) and a level should be marked on the rod at 6¼". If there is a considerable loss of oil in the pins this will need to be replenished on a more regular basis, or new seals fitted.

Check front brake pads (late P4's) before every M.O.T. and replace if worn down to about ⅛". Also prior to M.O.T. remove rear brake drums and examine slave cylinders for fluid seepage, if any. Remove plate from rear of cylinders and clean the sliders and rollers on the handbrake mechanism. Regrease. Spray all pivot points of hand brake with WD40. Adjust brake shoes.

Every two years change oil in back axle and gearbox. This level should be checked on the dipstick every couple of months.

Check brake fluid level every week when car is used regularly. Once a year spray door locks with WD40.

It helps to keep a record of maintenance and mileages and with a bit of careful planning all these jobs can be spread out through the year.

Stan Johnstone   *1991 Yearbook*

BRAKING POINT

As Technical Advisor for the Guild I get asked many questions on the mechanics of the P4. By far the most popular query is concerning bleeding the brake system. Many members have found that it is not always a simple case of pumping the air out into a bottle. The most common problem occurs after refitting the master cylinder albeit a replacement unit or the original with new seals. What many fail to do is to prime the master cylinder with fluid before fitting. This is done by carefully pouring a small amount of brake fluid into the inlet hole on the top of the cylinder and gently actuating the push rod until fluid is flowing from the outlet hole. Be very careful of your eyes when carrying this out!

Once the cylinder is full of fluid refit to the car. Always use new fluid on refilling the system and bleed the brakes in the normal sequence i.e. back nearside, back offside, front nearside and finally front offside. Of course the most easy and effective way to bleed the system is to use an 'Easi-bleed' kit made by Gunsons. With this you can do the job on your own (without bothering the wife) and not touch the brake pedal at all. The kit simply takes pressure from the spare tyre (let down to about 20 p.s.i.) and pressurises the fluid reservoir. With the kit you get a selection of caps to fit the reservoir. There is one very near to the Rover size but I have used a spare one from a

P4 and drilled a hole in it to fit the adaptor supplied. This is safer because you do not want to run the risk of spraying brake fluid all over the off-side wing! The 'Easi-bleed' costs about £12 from Halfords and is well worth the cost.

Another question often asked is how to get the handbrake to D.O.T. standards. Generally this is achieved by checking that the rear slave cylinders are free to move on the back-plate. Invariably they are seized solid to the plate and will not allow the brake shoes to centralise. This is easily rectified by removing the rear brake cylinders and wire brushing the brake back-plate inside and out along with the small plate which the nuts and special spring washers tighten onto. Grease both sides of the back-plate and fit the cylinders systematically, tightening the three nuts until it is held against the back-plate but is still able to slide up and down in the slots. Clean and replace the hand brake drawlinks, tappets and rollers and grease with copper-slip. Check that the balance lever on the rear-axle is set to the correct angle and not pulling against itself and you should then have a good handbrake to keep you and the tester happy.

Stan Johnstone

1991 Yearbook

REAR ENGINE MOUNTING – REPLACEMENT PROCEDURE

Of all the technical enquiries I receive, one of the most often asked is how to replace the rear engine mounting. Yes, it is called the rear engine mounting, not the rear gearbox mounting as it is often erroneously called, because, whilst it is the only support the gearbox has, apart from being bolted to the back of the engine, without it the engine would have only the front two mounts to hold it in place.

This very important component works very hard for a living and has an immense stress imposed upon it. Its greatest enemy is oil which destroys the molecular structure of the rubber encasing it. Rear crankshaft oil seals and top rocker cover gaskets are the main culprits. When it is of an age, the mounting loses its strength, allowing the engine and gearbox to become liberated developing that well known shudder, particularly when pulling away from rest or reversing.

Make sure that the front engine mounts are in good order first. To check these, gently try to jack up the engine from the front whilst watching the mounting rubbers. Once under load, they should show no sign of being split or broken. If you have established that they are alright, you will have to replace the rear engine mounting. Tackle the job thus:

i) Remove the front seat(s), carpet, gear-change mechanism and gearbox cover. You should now be looking at the gearbox in all its glory.

ii) Now get under the bonnet, remove the top hose, throttle linkage from the carburettor, and separate the exhaust manifold from the down pipe.

iii) Ensure the car is safely supported for you to clamber underneath, I use heavy blocks of wood approximately 12" high under the front wheels as I always like to have the car standing on its own feet as it were. You can, of course, use axle stands. Make sure that the rear wheels are chocked and please, please, take the utmost care, many people have been squashed, many fatally, whilst working on the underside of cars.

iv) Drain the gearbox oil . . . . . completely.

v) Under the car, remove prop-shaft from rear flange of the gearbox/free-wheel (dependent on model) and remove rear engine mounting bolt from mounting and chassis. Undo the clutch cross shaft from the side of the gearbox and (if fitted) remove the overdrive solenoid from the overdrive unit.

vi) Gently jack up the engine at the point where the gearbox bolts to the engine, I use a block of wood with a vee sawn into it so that it stays central during lifting, until the top studs holding the gearbox to the rear of the engine are just touching the apex of the aperture in the bulkhead.

At this point the gearbox will be sitting up into the interior of the car.

vii) Undo the nuts and bolts holding the extension casing to the rear face of the gearbox. Ensure that you only split it at this point and not where the overdrive or free-wheel joins the extension casing. (It is the extension casing that houses the rear mounting on overdrive models, the tail-shaft housing on non-overdrive models and in the free-wheel unit on models so fitted).

On free-wheel models the ferrule holding the free-wheel cable must be removed to allow the unit to be pulled away from the gearbox.

On overdrive models it is vital that the isolator switch is withdrawn from the extension casing. Make sure that the plunger inside it is removed, this is activated by the 3rd and 4th speed selector shaft and if it is not removed you will find it impossible to slide the unit back on to the gearbox when you have fitted the mounting and are putting it back together.

viii) Slide the unit away from the gearbox.

(As an aside, I always remove this unit first when removing a gearbox as the two lumps are, obviously, lighter separately. It makes the refitting of the gearbox easier. In my younger days, sigh, I used to do it in one lump. Now I like to make life as stress free as possible).

ix) Spread newspapers on the dining room table before you take the unit inside to remove the old mounting. Cut out the rubber, using a very sharp knife and hacksaw, a slot along the width of the outer sleeve until the blade just meets with the aluminium of the casing, the sleeve will then literally lose its grip and will be easy to tap out. You will definitely damage the casing if you do not split the rubber first.

The mounting is an unbelievable seven thou interference fit which is tighter than anything I am allowed to mention in this publication. The outside diameter of the mounting is 2.255" plus .002" and the hole in the casing is 2.250" minus .002", so to fit these two into each other would be impossible at a common temperature.

x) You should place the new mounting in a plastic bag and place it in the coldest compartment of your freezer for, preferably, 24 hours prior to fitting. Clean out the bore of the casing and gently heat the area around the hole using a blow lamp but make sure you keep the heat localised. When the aluminium is really hot insert the frozen mounting with the eccentric hole on the centre line and to the base of the unit. Quickly tap in the mounting using a copper mallet until it is fully home. (Strong industrial gloves are needed to protect your hands from the two extremes of temperature).

xii) Allow everything to cool down, including yourself, and you are then ready to put the whole lot back together again. As they say in all the best workshop manuals, "sling it all back together in reverse order".

A lot of work for such a small component but well worth the effort when, once again, you pull away from rest as every Rover should.

Stan Johnstone   *1997 Yearbook*

BARREL LOCKS BY THE TECHNOCRAT

Good old Wilmot Breeden, some of those locks on our favourite motors have been working for a very long time. But, have you ever had to replace a barrel and are frustrated that you now have to carry one key for the door and one key for the ignition? Would you like to have them both the same with no greater cost than a little patience? Then read on for the technocrat has the answer.

How does it work?

In an efficient lock in good repair, the barrel proper is able to rotate either a quarter or a half turn within the outer casing but is prevented by doing so by the five tumblers that are spring loaded to engage in a slot within the outer casing unless the correct key is inserted. Each tumbler has a rectangular slot and one end, the "acting face", is at a calibrated distance from the tumbler end.

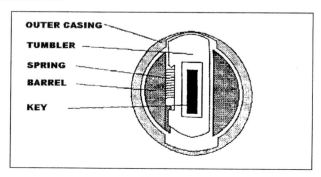

Figure 1

When the correct key is inserted, the part of the key in line with each tumbler exerts pressure so that the tumbler is flush with the outside of the barrel on each side so that the barrel is able to rotate. See Fig. 1

An incorrect key will move the tumbler but either too far or not far enough thereby preventing rotation.

So, what goes wrong?

The most common problem is with sticking. Oh, a squirt of WD40 will cure it for a little while but it will wash out the actual lubricant and it will freeze in winter. The body of the barrel is made of our old friend Mazac (zinc alloy) and the tumblers are of brass or plated steel. Whaddya get with mis-matched metals? Electrolytic corrosion. So, you need a coating of grease to keep them apart.

Removal for lubrication

The barrel is held into its housing by a latch which resembles an extra tumbler.

Once the lock has been removed a small hole will be visible into which can be inserted a scriber to push back the latch. Occasionally, a barrel will fall out because the latch has fallen out or is simply stuck.

On dis-assembly, carefully wash all the parts, grease well and re-assemble.

Making a barrel fit a different key

Right, you have obtained a replacement barrel and you want to make it fit your old key. It will help if you have a supply of old lock barrels, or you may get away with fitting the tumblers from the barrel you want to replace.

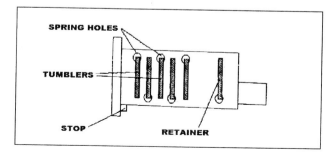

Figure 2

Wash all the bits and remove the tumblers.

Locate the side of the barrel where the spring holes are visible, we will call this the top for the sake of convenience. Fig. 2

The tumblers can now be pushed out from the bottom with a small screwdriver. Work over some sort of container, you are unlikely to find a spring if it falls on your garage floor. Repeat the process on the old lock or any scrap barrels you may have to supply a set of tumblers.

Now, insert the key and one tumbler at a time by inserting them upside down in the bottom of the barrel. You are looking for those with action faces that fall flush with the barrel. Fig. 3

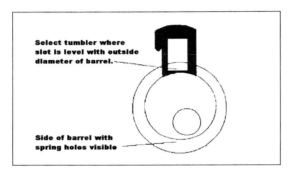

Figure 3

Each time you find a tumbler, remove the key and fit the tumbler to the barrel. A tip is to smear the tumbler with grease and insert so that the spring slot is half in. Then insert the spring, lower end first, gently compress it and engage the top on the triangular projection in the slot. Push the tumbler in and when the key is once again inserted the tumbler should, of course, be flush. Repeat this until all the tumblers have been inserted.

Smear the assembly with grease and re-fit.

It really isn't as complicated as it sounds and is much easier to do than to write about! It is possible to leave out a tumbler but this will be at the expense of security.

Anon.   *Yearbook 1997*

IS AN UNLEADED CONVERSION NECESSARY FOR A P4?

Firstly, only you can decide whether to do any remedial work, or just wait until the issue is forced upon you, and you just have no choice but to address the problem. Personally, I think the latter option is the best bet. As I have said before, why fix it 'til it's broke? I, like many P4 drivers, have taken the plunge and have been using unleaded fuel without preparing the engine in any way. If you are going down this road, I think the prudent thing to do though is to make regular checks on the tappet clearances, especially the exhaust valves. These should be set very carefully before you start using unleaded. These exhaust clearances are best checked when the engine is 'overnight' cold, but the inlets must be set or checked with the engine at full working temperature, i.e. after at least a thirty mile run. By monitoring these clearances at regular intervals, you can keep an eye on any valve/valve seat recession that may or may not be occurring.

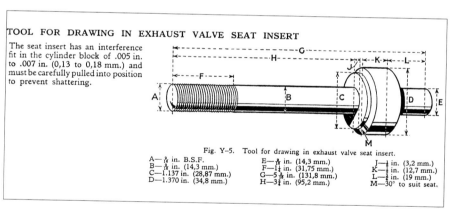

TOOL FOR DRAWING IN EXHAUST VALVE SEAT INSERT

The seat insert has an interference fit in the cylinder block of .005 in. to .007 in. (0,13 to 0,18 mm.) and must be carefully pulled into position to prevent shattering.

Fig. Y–5.   Tool for drawing in exhaust valve seat insert.

A—⅝ in. B.S.F.
B—⅝ in. (14,3 mm.)
C—1.137 in. (28,87 mm.)
D—1.370 in. (34,8 mm.)

E—⅝ in. (14,3 mm.)
F—1¼ in. (31,75 mm.)
G—5⅛ in. (131,8 mm.)
H—3¾ in. (95,2 mm.)

J—⅛ in. (3,2 mm.)
K—½ in. (12,7 mm.)
L—¾ in. (19 mm.)
M—30° to suit seat.

If, however, you would prefer peace of mind and feel inclined to embark on an unleaded conversion, I will relate to you the correct way to go about it. The main components that will have to be changed are the exhaust valves themselves. The main Rover partsmen now have these in stock (but for how long I don't know, so it might be worth putting a set on the wine rack!) they have a high stainless steel content and are up for the job. The valve seats for the exhaust are capable of coping without lead, but must be in first class condition, i.e. no surface cracks. If they show any signs of wear they will have to be changed, and if so, you will invariably have to change the exhaust guides too, because once the new seat is installed, its face will have to be cut and the cutting tool uses the guide as its pilot. An old worn guide will not allow a concentric face to be cut. Removing the guides is relatively easy, using the appropriate drift (see diagram), but seat removal is not so easy. Ideally the seat will have to be weakened by using an air drill with a small grinding burr fitted. Extra care must be taken in this procedure, working at the top of the seat furthest away from the cylinder bore. Once the seat has been virtually ground through, it can then be broken using a good quality, sharp chisel. Wear your goggles for this job! The seat recess can then be cleaned out thoroughly, ready for the new seat to be fitted. These seats are very hard and of a brittle nature, so the only way to fit them is using a pulling tool as shown in the diagram. The new seats should be pulled in when the guides are removed, and once fitted, the new guides can be drifted in ready for the new seats to be cut. You can then lap the new SS exhaust valves into their mating seats.

You can then concentrate on the other half, namely the cylinder head. I have covered this topic in Yearbook 1992, so will not go over it all again. If you haven't got that particular article, send me an SAE and I will send you a photocopy of it.

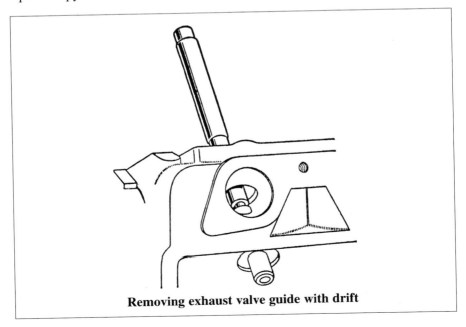

Removing exhaust valve guide with drift

To sum up, as regards the head, it is essential to have the face surface ground to zero flatness and most certainly not 'skimmed' as most companies would do, as it will not end up flat and the surface finish will not be fine enough to prevent 'gassing'.

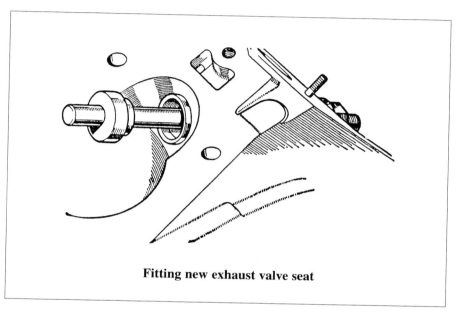

Fitting new exhaust valve seat

It will be well worth replacing the inlet valves guides and recutting the seats. Inlet valves are not expensive to buy as opposed to exhaust valves, so it makes sense to buy new and lap them in to the recut seats. Do not forget to fit new 'O' seals to the inlet guides. When replacing the inlet rocker gear into the cylinder head, it is wise to replace the inlet rocker spacers (x3), so that the rockers sit centrally over the valve stems.

Once all this preparation has been done, you are then set for some unleaded motoring, but before you do, you will have to give some thought to the cooling system.

The engine will run hotter on unleaded fuel, but this shouldn't be a problem if the system is up to par. The P4 engine in fact, was overcooled if anything, but that could be as long as fifty years ago, or as short as thirty-five years ago, depending on the model, so it is fair to say that some silting, and thus congestion, will have occurred. for complete peace of mind, it would be an opportune time to remove the core plugs along the side of the engine block and with the use of a power hose, thoroughly flush the block, paying particular attention to the rear of the block. Since the P4 engine sits lower at the back than the front, it is very prone to silting, and being furthest from the fan does tend to run much hotter at the rear, because of the lack of coolant circulation going round the rear cylinder jackets. A good poke round with some sturdy wire should encourage a bit of descaling to take place, with the use of the power hose. When you are happy that the block is a lot cleaner than it was, new core plugs can be fitted.

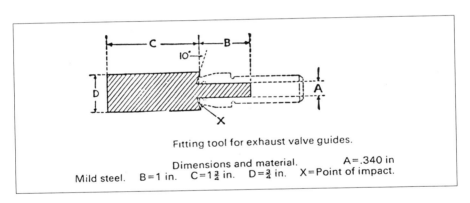

Fitting tool for exhaust valve guides.

Dimensions and material. A = .340 in
Mild steel.   B = 1 in.   C = 1¾ in.   D = ¾ in.   X = Point of impact.

Radiators are invariably furred up and therefore not as efficient as they should be, so a radiator specialist can run a flow test on it and at the worst, may advise a new core. Expensive maybe, but if it means you can carry on driving your P4 for many years to come, it's money well spent.

That's it, that's all you need to do to your Rover, in order to drive it way beyond the millennium.

Stan Johnstone   *1999 Yearbook*

INSIDE INFORMATION

I have never been particularly impressed by the handbrake on my P5 which although similar to the P4 is operated by an umbrella handle and cable rather than a proper lever. I assumed the reason for this poor performance was the bedding in of new linings and the lack of a proper lever.

Recently however, things took a turn for the worse after a rear brake service when the hand brake failed to hold the car on hills – necessitating working three pedals with two feet to avoid rolling back into the car behind.

The shoes had been aligned in the drums and steady posts adjusted in accordance with the workshop manual and all the operating rods and levers were correctly adjusted. Fortunately Colin and Anne Blowers visited one afternoon so I took the opportunity to get a fresh mind on the problem. After much investigation Colin noticed that the nearside handbrake draw link was pulling through to its stop when the handbrake was applied although the drum could still be rotated.

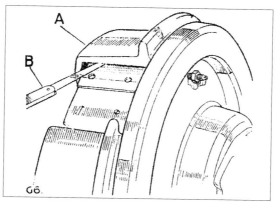

Again the drums were removed and Colin realised that the shoes were lying close to the backplate and as a result of this the linings were only contacting the drum on this outside edge. A readjustment of the steady posts resulted in a vastly improved handbrake and incidentally much reduced footbrake travel.

Having originally adjusted the steady posts in accordance with the manual I cannot understand why the shoes were so far out of alignment. I have had no problems of this nature with my P4.

I have since cut a section out of the circumference of an old drum which when fitted in place of the normal drum enables a feeler gauge to be used on the inner and outer edges of the lining thus enabling the steady posts and shoes to be adjusted with great accuracy. I now have a handbrake almost as effective as the P4.

Derek Humphreys   **2000 Yearbook**

BACKLIGHT

This photo shows how the glass frame seal, frame and body seal fit together. The whole assembly complete with frame and body seal is pulled against the edge of the body recess by clips and shims screwed to the car body from inside as shown later.

Whenever I have sought advice about removing the backlight, the almost unanimous reply has been "Don't mess with it". Unfortunately for me this advice had come too late. So for those of you who must, here are some tips.

There are definitely "two levels of hell" when it comes to the backlight.

The first level of backlight hell is when you remove the frame complete from the car, fit a new body rubber to it, and then refit the whole unit back to the car. When removing the backlight from the car always make a note of how many shims are used under each clip, since you are likely to use the same number when re-fitting it.

The worst problem that I found during re-fitting was that the new seal was a different section to the original. At first I thought that the differences were not significant, however the combined effect of the shallower curve at the top left where the frame presses it against the car, meant that the feathered edge would not sit against the body no matter how I tried. At the National I did some research, and ascertained that all the sections on offer by the spares men were essentially the same. I also talked to someone who had used one of the rubbers who said that he'd had to resort to gluing the edge down.

When fitting this seal to the frame it is easiest to hook the heel into the square part of the frame slot all the way round the frame first. Lubricate the crevice between the back of the heel and the frame (I used special Hellerine rubber lubricant for this, which is available from Electrospeed. You will have to phone them, because their website is awkward to use! The stock number is 254-62063D). Carefully work the seal into the frame with a blunt screwdriver.

This picture isn't very clear, sorry.

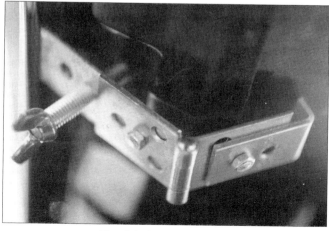

Here it is in position. . . . . .

. . . . . and here is one of the others in position. You can see one of the retainers that hooks under the edge of the frame, on the left of the clamp. Notice the shakeproof washer. This one doesn't have any shims behind it. The self tapping screws are of different lengths, so it's a good idea to poke something into the hole first to make sure there is enough depth available, otherwise you could distort the outer body skin as you tighten the screw.

The next problem I encountered was that the clamps have never been available so I decided it was probably easiest to make up a set. As you can see they're crudely made, but they work. I found that galvanised building ties are the cheapest source of suitable metal and the holes are conveniently just the right size to be tapped out to 8mm without extra drilling. The leverage is better when the wing-bolt is nearer the hooked end of the clamp, but the variation shown was acceptable. It is well worth making an extra couple of the top ones, because I ended up grouping the clamps together in places to get enough leverage.

The ones for the bottom at the sides are the same dimensions as those for the top, but need to be twisted. The bottom centre one is the most difficult to make, and has a prong that goes into the hole under the centre of the window aperture.

When fitting the backlight I put a bead of Evo-Stik Frame and Gutter

Sealant round the lip of the body aperture before offering up the frame. This not only seals the join but allows the whole thing to slide into position more easily. It is a rubberised bitumen sealant and is closer to the original type than anything else I have found, also the excess can be removed with white spirit. I do not like silicone because if you ever have to take the window out again you can never get the stuff off satisfactorily without wrecking the paintwork. Getting the window to fit is a terrible job made worse by the fact that the retaining clips are screwed to the single inner skin of the body with self tappers, which may strip if excessive strain is placed on them. Use the clamps, levers, bad language and any other means at your disposal to pull the frame into position as described in the workshop manual. I would suggest getting the sides to fit nicely first, while watching the gap between the body and frame all the way round, and sharing out the free play, if any. You will find that if you pull the frame too far into the car the feathered edge of the seal will pivot away from the body. This may seem counter intuitive at first.

Once the sides are looking reasonable, put in some of the retaining clips in this area using shims as required tightening lightly, then turn your attention to the top and bottom edges. Do not be afraid to lever things carefully. Be prepared to start again. And again, until it looks right. When you have got it right, go out and celebrate!

The second level of backlight hell comes when you decide to dismantle the frame itself.

It is in two halves which are joined by straps in the glass recess with 4 screws each side. The bottom screws are likely to be rusted solid. The glass sits in a slot in the frame, cushioned, and hopefully (some hope) sealed by a U-section of pitch impregnated fibrous stuff. You can see this in the first photo at the beginning of this article. The sections of glass are joined by an H shaped rubber extrusion. Before you dismantle the frame, be warned, read the rest of this first!

For the U section the nearest seems to be section R250 from Woolies.

The inherent difficulty of assembling the frame being surmountable, the real obstacle lies with vertical strips. The original section is shown at the bottom. The section at the top is offered as a replacement by all the spares men. They claim that they've sold many and never had any complaints, but as you can see it is really intended for joining much thinner material, and I have never seen one used in anger. The really bad news is that I have not been able to find a source of anything that is better. It may be possible to fabricate something suitable out of T section, but in my opinion it is not currently possible to rebuild the backlight satisfactorily without re-using the original strips, so if you're determined to dismantle the frame, be very careful not to damage them, bearing in mind that they may have become brittle over the years.

Please e-mail me if you've tried the new section or found a better replacement.

The "Cheat Method" for Fixing Glass to Frame Leaks

With so many problems to overcome, I decided not to dismantle my backlight frame, but try and reseal it while still assembled...

I dug out some of the original fibrous seal between the outer surface of the glass and the frame, taking care not to scratch anything of course. Then I cleaned out the furrow with a brush. Next I ran two strips of masking tape round the window, one up to the lip of the frame and the other parallel on the glass, leaving a gap that I could work "U-Pol Tiger Seal" into using my finger without smearing it all over the frame or glass. This is a really first class sealer with superb adhesion, which hardens into a flexible rubber-like material. I carried the masking tape over the vertical strips so that sealant could be worked into the corners of the join to try and ensure a watertight seal. Removing the tape is a bit time consuming, but it really does save time in the long run. I found this method stopped all the leaks, but I think it is best used once the frame is back on the car and it has had time to settle, so that subsequent movement is kept to a minimum.

Roger Dealtry http://www.p4.org.uk   **2000 Yearbook**

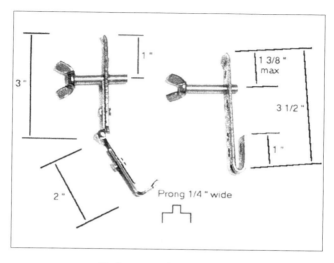

66. fittings tools for backlight

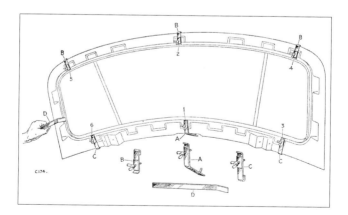

The complete set of tools as listed below are essential when fitting the three-piece backlight on the Rover car.

Part Numbers: Models:

Type 'A' 314322 1 off   1955-57 '60', '75', '90'
Type 'B' 314029 3 off   and '105'
Type 'C' 314371 2 off
Type 'D' 314385 1 off

Numbers on illustration indicate the sequence in which to fit the clamp brackets when commencing to reassemble back light.

Taken from Rover Workshop Tools January 1957

I'VE BEEN FRAMED

Following on from Roger Dealtry's "Backlight" article in the Guild's 2000 Yearbook, I present you with a résumé of my experience of this dreaded task. For me the removal of my 1960 '100's rear window was not an option; the chrome frame was pitted, a bare metal respray was planned and the external rubber was brittle and breaking up. Having never dealt with the removal and replacement of a P4 rear window I employed a contractor to remove it for me. This was mistake number 1 as I did not see the number of shims required for each rear window bracket, more about this later. The next mistake was to employ the same contractor to refit the rear window, he had not done the job before and I ended up with the 3 glass sections sitting in silicon sealant and an incomplete job. I thought long and hard about what to do and fortunately chanced upon Roger's excellent P4 web site and the informative article on the rear window.

Refitting the glass into the Frame

Until I read Roger's article I had no awareness of the rubber u-section surrounding the edge of the three rear glass sections within the frame. On dismantling my rear window all I found was hard black stuff of an indeterminate nature and I assumed it was just old sealant. Anyway, Roger's article identified the R250 U-section from Woolies as being suitable so I went ahead and ordered the required length.

I decided that the dining table extended to its six foot length, suitably protected, was just right for the job and managed to convince my wife Jean of the merits of this approach; it was in the warm, the right size to work on and at the right height! Also closer to the kitchen for much needed refreshments.

The two new sections of the vertical rubber strip that separates the three glass sections had to be trimmed to the right length so I assembled the window frame to assess the required length. Unfortunately I measured the internal dimension and not the external dimension which is slightly longer and shaped to accommodate the profile of the chrome frame. Check a P4 before you attempt this to see what I mean. Because of this I have needed to prepare a small in-fill section for my car using some of the surplus I cut off. The R250 will not sit neatly around the corners of the glass and fit within the frame so Jean, using her sewing skills, cut small vee-shaped sections out of the rubber to help.

The logistics of aligning and sliding the 3 pieces of glass, 2 rubber strips and the R250 within the bottom section of the frame would have been a sight to behold. Both Jean and I struggled initially with the frame on the table and then on the floor to align and push the various components together, aided by Fairy Liquid for lubrication. I also put a small bead of the Evo-Stik Roof and Gutter Sealant into the frame as an added measure for water tightness. Unfortunately, this made matters slightly worse as the surplus sealant had to squeeze past the glass edged with R250 as the components were pushed together. Miraculously getting all the components lined up into the bottom section of the frame was not too difficult with the middle section of glass coming adrift just twice; this necessitated starting the process again.

Having dealt with the bottom half of the frame the time came for the top half. But at this point don't forget to fit the two metal strips that hold the two sections of the frame together. They fit internally within the frame with the four small screws being driven in from the outside of the frame. Fitting the top section of the frame was not too difficult as the glass sections were being held in more or less the correct position by the bottom half of the frame. However, on pushing the top section on the glass edged by R250 it became apparent that with normal force the two sections were about half a centimetre apart. This is where the project would have become a contender for the TV programme "You've Been Framed" as both Jean and me grappled with the framed window in all manner of positions on the dining room floor pushing with all our might. There is something about the shape of the rear window frame that makes it unsuitable for heaving it together. I tried to think of alternative means of forcing it together but in the absence of anything realistic continued to push down on the frame on the floor with all my strength, hoping that the glass would not crack.

When it reached the point where I could put the final 2 screws in to the 2 joining strips I was jubilant that this stage was complete, little did I know what was to follow. At this point all that was left to do before the next stage of the project (a nightmare come true) was to trim off the surplus R250 showing around the edge of the chrome frame with a Stanley knife (Johnstone gets in everywhere!).

Fitting the external rubber to the frame

On inspecting the new rubber it was apparent that it was too long and would need to be shortened and joined. So with the manufactured join at the centre-top we proceeded to fit the rubber to the frame with a plan to make a cut and join at the centre-bottom. Using Roger's advice I utilised a blunt screwdriver to ease the rubber into the frame with some Fairy Liquid for lubrication. This is easier said than done as whilst it is quite easy to insert the rubber along the straight sections of the frame it is very difficult around the curved sections, especially the tightly curved top corners. Again the dining table came into its own and with Jean's help holding the frame at the right angle the task was slowly completed. Does anybody know how Rover did this on the production line? There must have been a special tool. The join in the rubber was achieved using Superglue and after allowing it to set the last section was inserted into the frame.

Fitting the complete rear window into the car

Nothing could have prepared me for this stage in the project. Fortunately I had been in contact with Roger through his website link and not being particularly practically minded to make a set of clamps for myself I decided to ask Roger if I could borrow his. I will be forever grateful to Roger for the loan of his clamps.

Using the advice in Roger's article I put a toothpaste size bead of Evo-Stick Roof and Gutter sealant around the aperture and levered (using a variety of implements, mainly a large screwdriver), clamped and swore. Jean stood outside the car giving a view on how flush the window appeared with respect to the car's bodywork. This procedure was made more difficult because I had no record of the number of shims required for each bracket owing to the rear window being removed by the contractor. However, after much effort the window was in but it proved impossible to get the bottom near-side corner to fit neatly and flush with the shape of the surrounding bodywork. So I removed the whole frame! The amount of leverage necessary to pull the frame into the aperture also seemed excessive to me and I was really concerned that I was doing something very wrong. This being especially of concern when some of Roger's clamps started to bend with all the tension.

Having cleaned the sealant off with white spirit we had another go and this time the self tapping screw holes for a couple of the brackets stripped! So I went up a size of screw. Unfortunately, the amount of screwing and unscrewing stripped the holes again. Fortunately Rover provided enough space around the space where the brackets fit to enable a new hole to be drilled. Imagine drilling in this area with the potential to drill through the external skin of a car which has just had a bare metal respray! Unfortunately, for a second time it proved impossible to position the near-side bottom corner correctly.

I decided to undo the brackets, clean the frame up and seek some moral support and guidance from Roger. After a very long telephone conversation with Roger and further discussion with other Essex Branch members I decided that I would have another attempt. To my horror, on looking at the rubber seal, I noticed that cracks were beginning to appear at the corners! I assumed that this might have been as a result of cleaning up the frame with white spirit so I purchased a new seal and started the complete process again! Should white spirit have done this to the rubber?

This time I got as far as inserting the new rubber into the frame and a variety of events occurred that resulted in a few months of no work on the car. On hearing the disastrous tales at Essex Branch meetings one of the members, Jason Dorey, kindly offered to give me a hand. We agreed a convenient date, however, two days before this date I noticed that the corners of the new seal were starting to crack. So we delayed the task until I purchased another seal. I began to wonder if the rubber was not flexible enough to bend around the corners of the frame. During the intervening period I looked at Jason's P4, a 1962 '100' with its original window rubber. It was apparent that the original seals had a greater amount of external rubber to fit against the external bodywork of the car. I discussed the matter with a different supplier and arranged to pick a new rubber up at the 2001 National Rally. The rally also allowed me to have a good look at P4 rear windows. So apologies to those of you who were alarmed by some bearded bloke gazing at your car's rear window, I was making an assessment of the shape of the external rubber seal and also the alignment with the surrounding bodywork.

Two things arose from this casual investigation. Firstly, it is definite that the original window rubbers have a more generous external section of rubber providing more rubber for the frame to sink into externally. Secondly, even cars with original fit rear windows do not always have frames that are completely flush with the line of the bodywork all the way around the aperture.

So armed with this added information I fitted the new rubber to the frame. The first thing I noticed was that the profile of the new rubber's section that fits into the frame was thicker and this made fitting the rubber extremely difficult around the corners. However, the additional external profile looked very promising. The moment then came to fit the blighter...

Jason and myself found a convenient date and the battle lines were drawn, this window was going in and that was that! We went through the same process as before and after much joint effort the window was in. The near-side bottom corner was again not flush with the bodywork as it was impossible to achieve this with all other parts of the frame in the correct place. However, with the more generous external profile of the seal this did not matter so much. Unfortunately, the rubber seal was not flush with the bodywork at the nearside bottom corner and required being stuck to the bodywork, this would have not been needed with a more generous external profile of rubber.

Key points for the whole process:
- Roger's article is a priceless guide to the process.
- Make a note of the number of shims required for each window bracket before removing your rear window.
- Do not expect perfect alignment with the surrounding bodywork, adjust the position of the window frame with the clamps and levering until you obtain the best overall fit.
- Somebody needs to manufacture a rear window rubber seal that is a combination of the inner section of the first type I purchased with the outer section of the second type I purchased. I think that a larger section of external rubber to meet with the external bodywork is required.

I would like to thank the following people for all their help in what for me was the hardest task I can remember:

- Jean for helping me during the winter months, she was wrapped in several layers of clothes to keep warm in the freezing cold garage, during my initial attempts. She certainly heard some colourful words that until that time she probably didn't think I had in me!

- Roger for his article, the loan of his clamps and the moral support.
- Jason for his help during the final onslaught.

It may be that you would not have encountered the above difficulties but I hope my experience helps you in some way. I would be more than happy to give moral support to anybody considering the battle of their rear window. Please contact Stan Johnstone for my details.

And finally, if you need to do the same job you have my sympathy!

Eamonn Burnell

2001 Yearbook

THE OFT FORGOTTEN STEERING RELAY

Of all the parts on the P4 chassis that seem to get the least attention at service time, I think the steering relay (or Idler) unit must be it. How many of you remember to check the oil level, if indeed there is one! Very often the seal has given up trying to keep the oil in and the unit soon becomes empty and hence unlubricated, causing rapid wear in the bushes. The MOT tester seems to enjoy finding excessive play in this unit, but at the same time isn't generally interested in putting the matter right because of the labour involved.

Ideally, to tackle the job thoroughly, the relay will have to be removed from the car. Do not concern yourself with trying to remove the drop-arm from its main spindle, as this very often does not want to be removed unless you possess a very substantial hydraulic puller. Just release the track-rod joints from it and leave it still attached to the unit. The bolts holding the relay unit to the chassis are, generally speaking, very stubborn and will require a good soaking in a releasing agent such as Plus-Gas. The bolts tend to corrode in the aluminium casting of the relay unit body.

Once removed from the chassis, the unit can be stripped of all its components. Start by removing the oil filler plug, which will reveal a circlip just inside the body. After removing the circlip, the shaft can be pressed out of the collar, downwards, out of the bottom of the relay unit. Again the collar can be reluctant to break its fit with the shaft and ideally a press should be used to gently get it on the move. If a press isn't available, a brass drift and a heavy hammer can be employed.

Carefully prise out the seal from the base of the housing. Clean all the parts and then try the shaft back inside the bushes to detect for any wear. Hopefully there will be no perceptible movement, but if there is, the bushes will have to be pressed out and new ones fitted.

If new bushes are fitted, make sure there is absolutely no tightness when the shaft is installed. If there is any interference between shaft and bushes, they will have to be carefully reamed out. The end-float (i.e. up and down movement) is controlled by the shoulder of the top bush and the collar and circlip groove. Ideally you should have .002" / .003" thou. end-float (.05 / .07 mm). If this cannot be achieved you can carry out the modification which is detailed in the Rover Workshop manual. This will require the oil-filler plug to be drilled and tapped ¼" BSF. A good quality high textile 1½" x ¼" BSF hexagon head bolt will have to be used in this modification. A 'soft' bolt will wear very rapidly, so make sure to use a 'Rover' type quality bolt. Do not forget to saw a slot across the hexagon for the bolt to allow oil to enter the idler shaft. Also cut one in the end of the thread to facilitate the use of a screwdriver for adjustment of the end float. Once the relay is bolted back onto the chassis (don't forget to use copper-slip grease on the mounting bolts) and the track-rod ends are attached, the end-float can be adjusted by turning the bolt down on to the shaft unit it just touches and then tighten the lock nut. Use 90 EP oil in the unit which hopefully, after all your labour, will not trickle out past the seal!

This little job should keep you on the straight and narrow providing of course, there is not any other wear existing in the steering box, swivel pins and track-rod ends.

Stan Johnstone   *1994 Yearbook*

THE LOWLY MANIFOLD

The exhaust manifolds of the P4 may seem to most of you, to be a pretty basic piece of Rover engineering to warrant a mention in your Yearbook, but believe me, when I tell you, that there is a lot to be learned about the lowly P4 manifold.

Produced for The Rover Company by Qualcast, a business more famously known for producing lawnmowers, the ignominious exhaust manifold, barely got more than a sentence of mention in the workshop manual, but in fact, has quite a bit of explaining to do for itself!

Fundamentally, there are six types of manifold fitted to the P4 range:– the '75/90', '60', '80', '105', '100/95' and '110'. They were all 1¾" bore, apart from the '105' and '110' which are 2" bore. The '60' has now become the dodo of all of them and is practically extinct, a rarity indeed. Whatever model you run, it makes sense to locate a spare for the future. When they have finally got used (or abused), they will be a difficult and expensive part to re-manufacture.

Theoretically, they should last forever, but like almost everything else on this planet, it gets touched by man and therefore gets maltreated. How could you maltreat an exhaust manifold, I hear you say. Well, you can, quite simply by over tightening. The problem is, once the manifold is removed from the engine block, it releases its stresses of being firstly overtightened and then of course, heated and cooled infinitum, and relaxes, as it were, into a state where the mating faces are out of flatness in relation to each other. If you were to lay the manifold on to a flat surface, you would see quite a few gaps. The only real way to fit a manifold is to machine these faces into a common plane. Once this is done, it can be lightly clamped back on to the engine block. The secret of it all, is in the design of the clamps, which are cleverly designed, so that they only make line contact with the manifold. If you look at the end view of a clamp, you will see that it has a radius built into its base, so that it makes contact along its centre line. I see quite a high proportion of P4's with their clamps actually fitted upside down with the circular bosses, which are of course, the 'land' for the washer and nut to sit squarely on, facing the block.

The '80' manifold is a different set-up entirely, whereby the inlet manifold is sandwiched between the exhaust manifold. These should ideally be bolted onto a 'tooling' block and machined as one, and are certainly not a DIY proposition, but should be done if you want a gas-tight seal.

Once the exhaust manifolds are machined flat, they only need to be lightly bolted to the block, so that on warming up, they are actually allowed to expand underneath the line contact of the clamps and again when the engine is cooling down after use. It is very common to see a manifold cracked because they have been clamped too tight and hence not allowed to move underneath the clamping areas.

So to sum up, if you cannot for one reason or another, have the manifold machined flat, then the only option you have is to overtighten the bolts, so as to get a seal and overcome the distortion, but of course, you then run the risk of cracking the manifold.

Stan Johnstone   *1998 Yearbook*